HOTELS
À LA CARTE

HOTELS
À LA CARTE

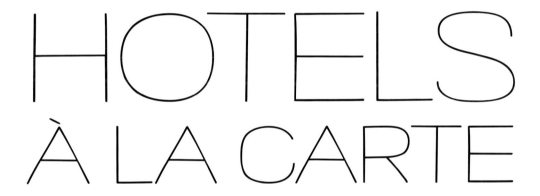

LANNOO

PROVENCE & CÔTE D'AZUR

LUC QUISENAERTS

PHOTOGRAPHY HENDRIK BIEGS

HOTELS À LA CARTE: PROVENCE AND CÔTE D'AZUR

Seldom have I seen so much variation, seldom have I made so many discoveries as I did on this excursion. And this applies both to scenic beauty and to gastronomy, culture and architecture. My journey took me south past Lyon. In a very brief period of time, the natural surroundings, the vegetation and the light changed before my eyes. I followed the banks of the Rhône and in the distance that majestic giant rose up in front of me: Mont Ventoux. Here I began my journey past wondrously beautiful 'farmhouses' with inviting swimming pools, past ancient monasteries and abbeys transformed into hotels, past castles and stately mansions. And wherever I went, I always found a place where I could relax under the plane trees or on a shady pavement to enjoy the magnificent landscape and the bright colours that still possess the same charm as when Gauguin, Van Gogh and Cézanne captured them on canvas. I found jewels of hotels, nestled and often hidden among the rocks of Les Alpilles, on the expansive plains of the Camargue, in the greenery and in the lavender meadows of the Luberon and in the shadow of the papal palace in Avignon. And on the idyllic peninsula of Saint-Tropez I visited southern bastides among vineyards and in subtropical gardens, and luxurious beach hotels at a stone's throw from the yacht harbour of Saint-Tropez. I concluded my journey on the Côte d'Azur, in the grandeur of the Belle-Époque: in Grand-Hôtel du Cap Ferrat, where I at any moment fancied that I could run into Charlie Chaplin, Gustave Eiffel or Picasso, a few of the many famous people who have contributed to the history of this hundred-year-old palace hotel.

Luc Quisenaerts

HOTELS À LA CARTE
PROVENCE & CÔTE D'AZUR

01

LA MIRANDE

In the Middle Ages, in the papal city of Avignon, the cardinals lived in villas as close as possible to the papal palace. After the fall of the popes, the cardinals also left Avignon, and the local French aristocracy moved into the magnificent houses.

One of the most beautiful residences is found in the historic part of the city on a paved square in the shadow of the papal palace. In 1990 these premises came into the possession of the Stein family. They dedicated themselves to the restoration and were able to retain the refinement and exclusivity of the interior. By recuperating old materials and doing a professional restoration, Martin Stein, the son in the family, restored the building to its former glory.

As soon as you walk through the entrance you find yourself in another world! You can admire valuable antique furniture, wall tapestries, paintings by old masters, frescos and the highly polished hardwood floors. The cardinal room, with its fourteenth-century ceiling, serves as the dining room.

The *Grand Salon* and the *Salon Napoléon III*, with its unique collection of porcelain, are breath-taking. In the evening, when the weather is nice, you can dine in the garden with the illuminated papal palace in the background.

A hotel guest once commented jokingly: *'If these elegant cardinal residences had been the residence of the pope rather than the monumental papal palace, not Rome, but Avignon would probably still be the seat of the Holy Roman Empire.'*

WITH THE CHEF'S OWN TOUCH...

CONFIT OF ROAST SHOULDER OF LAMB IN A BROWN SAVORY SAUCE

INGREDIENTS

For 4 people

Lamb juice

1 kg lamb scraps

10 cl groundnut oil

100 g carrots

100 g onion

1 clove of garlic

1 stalk of savory

50 g soft butter

salt and pepper

Confit of roast shoulder of lamb

8 cloves of garlic

4 small shoulders of suckling lamb

4 stalks of savory

10 cl olive oil

40 cl lamb juice

freshly ground salt and pepper

PREPARATION

Lamb juice

Cut the scraps of lamb into small pieces and braise them lightly in olive oil in a steel pan. Add the finely chopped carrot and onion, followed by the garlic, savory and butter. Allow to cook for a further 5 minutes, until the mixture reduces to a soft pulp. Remove from the heat and allow to drain. Deglaze by adding a small amount of water to the pan, so that any remaining bits of meat become loose. Season with the herbs. Cover the mixture in water and allow to simmer on a low heat for 2 hours, regularly skimming off any scum. Pass through a conical sieve and reduce by half, until the remaining fluid has a syrup-like consistency. Keep warm in a bain-marie.

Confit of roast shoulder of lamb

Peel the garlic and remove the core. Blanch three times. Season the shoulders and insert the cloves of garlic. Pack the shoulders into separate vacuum bags with a stalk of savory, a little olive oil and the lamb juice. Slow roast the shoulders for 36 hours in a steam oven at 67 °C.

Presentation

Make a garniture according to your preference: mushrooms, grenaille potatoes or seasonal vegetables. Glaze the shoulders of lamb with the cooking juices and colour them lightly under the grill. Place the meat in the middle of the plate and arrange the garnish around it. Serve with some of the lamb juice.

'My cooking is simple, authentic, rich and full of flavour.' In his never-ending search for authenticity and taste, François Secrétin has opted resolutely for the use of biologically-grown products, thereby lending his weight to those who are calling for a more ecological world. François' creative cooking is super-fresh and contains a number of Mediterranean influences. He maintains close and cordial relations with his suppliers and is constantly seeking to find the very best products, which are preferably home-grown and freshly picked at just the right moment of ripeness.

MORE
than just a hotel

....

WITH THE CHEF TO THE MARKET

With this formula you can go with one of the chefs of La Mirande to buy fish, meat, vegetables and fruit at the covered *'Les Halles d'Avignon.'* After that, together with the chef, you help to prepare the dishes in the nineteenth-century cellar kitchen of the cardinal's residence. The sommelier selects appropriate wines and provides information. In brief, this is an unforgettable experience for gastronomes.

....

WORTH DISCOVERING

Le Palais des Papes

The former cardinal's residence and the papal palace, the largest gothic construction in the world, are inseparably connected because of their common history. La Mirande is only a small street away from the imposing retreat of Pope Clemens V, who was expelled from Rome in 1306. At the beginning of the fifteenth century the popes returned to Rome.

The palace complex consists of two parts: the *Vieux Palais*, an imposing fortress with a monastery corridor, and the *Palais Neuf*, a building that radiates the power and wealth of the Catholic Church at that time. From the *Rocher des Doms*, the splendid gardens, you enjoy a magnificent view of the Rhône valley and the famous *Pont d'Avignon*.

02

LE PRIEURÉ

The little city of Villeneuve-les-Avignon lies on the right bank of the Rhône, on the other side from the historic city of Avignon. In the fourteenth century, which was the glory period of the papal empire, many cardinals had to move to the other side of the river because of a lack of space in Avignon. It had become easier to reach because of the now famous 'Pont d'Avignon.'

In 1322 cardinal Arnaud de Via, a nephew of Pope Jean XXII, had his palace built in the main street of Villeneuve. Before his death he gave his palace to nuns, who established a priory there. During the French Revolution the priory was sold as public property and served as a family boarding-house for entertainers. A certain Roger Mille purchased the complex in 1943 and under the Relais & Châteaux label, started a luxury hotel. In 2006 Jean-André Charial, the star chef of l'Oustau de Baumanière, took over Le Prieuré, increasing his influence in the luxury hotel world. Surrounded by luxuriant gardens full of roses and wisteria, the former priory has an exceptional charm. Geneviève Charial, Jean-André's wife, decorated the rooms, combining old with contemporary elements. When the weather is nice, meals are served in the pavement dining area among the magnificent gardens that at one time were maintained by nuns.

WITH THE CHEF'S OWN TOUCH...

POT-AU-FEU OF ERQUY SCALLOPS, FORGOTTEN VEGETABLES AND AUTUMN TRUFFLE

INGREDIENTS

For 4 people

Pot-au-feu

2 kg oxtail, cut into pieces
1 carrot
1 onion, laced with clove
1 leek
1 bouquet garni

Forgotten vegetables

1 kg kohlrabi
1 kg parsnip
500 g Hamburg parsley
500 g Vitelotte potatoes
300 g yellow carrot
200 g autumn truffle 'Tuber uncinatum'

Scallops

30 pieces

PREPARATION

Pot-au-feu

Colour the oxtail lightly, so that the stock turns a light amber colour. Mix with some chicken stock and allow to boil, skimming off any surface scum.
Add the aromatic garnish and the bouquet garni, and allow to simmer for at least 3 hours on a low heat.
Pass through a cloth, so that any impurities are removed. Keep to one side for later.

Forgotten vegetables

Chop all the vegetables to the desired level of fineness and boil them separately in the oxtail stock. Deglaze carefully and keep to one side for later.

Scallops

Remove the scallops from their shells, rinse them in very cold water, wrap them in a cloth and keep in a cool place.
Colour the scallops briefly on both sides in a little olive oil. Cook further for 1 or 2 minutes in the oven, depending on size. Add a knob of butter and season each individual scallop with a pinch of fleur de sel.

Presentation

Warm the vegetables and place them in a deep plate.
Place three scallops on each plate, together with three snippets of truffle.
Finish with some stock and serve immediately.

Fabien Fage, who once worked as an assistant in La Cabro d'Or, learned the tricks of the cooking trade in some of the world's great kitchens, such as those of Bernard Loiseau and Alain Ducasse.

His menu card betrays that his culinary roots are to be found in the Provence and Languedoc regions of Southern France.

During his years at La Cabro d'Or, he developed a preference for vegetables fresh from the garden plot and olive oil from Les Baux-de-Provence (AOC).

MORE
than just a hotel

. . . .

L'AFFECTIF

This wine is the creation of Jean-André Charial, owner of Le Prieuré. Eight thousand bottles are produced each year on the estate of Lauzières in Les Alpilles. The grapes are grown according to biodynamic principles. Thus, the soil and not the grapevines themselves are 'dynamised' or fed with homeopathic extracts of plants such as stinging nettles. The goal is to make the vines as resistant to moulds and diseases as possible.

. . . .

WORTH DISCOVERING

Châteauneuf-du-Pape

In the fourteenth century, Pope Johannes XXII decided to plant vineyards on the hills of his country house on the banks of the Rhône. It turned out to be a great success because at night the stony soil continued to give off the stored warmth from the sun, which enabled the grapes to ripen optimally. Because of the poor subsoil, the grapevines had to send their roots deep into the ground to find sufficient nutrition, which made them strong and resistant, and the vitamins found were transported directly to the grapes. This divine AOC wine is vinified on the basis of thirteen grape types, the main one being the *grenache*.

03

MAISON BRU

A stone's throw from Eygalières, a Provençal village at the foot of Les Alpilles, lies Maison Bru. This famous restaurant/hotel is the property of Wout and Suzy Bru, a Flemish couple who met at the hotel school in Bruges. In addition to being a popular television personality, Wout is also known as a star chef in Flanders and in other countries. Suzy is an energetic hostess who makes sure that her guests immediately feel at home.

The estate, that bathes in the aroma of thyme, lavender and mint, has an atmosphere of rest and refinement, and is located among magnificent vineyards and olive groves. The interior design is simple but beautiful, in balance with the natural character of the environment.

Although the construction style is typically Provençal, the simple interior and tasteful use of old materials give Maison Bru a Zen look that is carried over into the garden by means of the many modern works of art.

The nine rooms in bungalow style are distributed over the gardens or are located at the swimming pool.

Each has a pavement with much privacy.

WITH THE CHEF'S OWN TOUCH...

MARINATED TUNA WITH AN AVOCADO CREAM AND A SCALLOP CARPACCIO IN A SOYA VINAIGRETTE

INGREDIENTS

Marinated tuna

1 block, of tuna, 3 cm by 10 cm
1 litre balsamic vinegar
2 dl soya sauce, 1 dl olive oil
2 lemons, 10 g ginger
10 g garlic, 5 g peppercorns
80 g coriander seeds
500 g sugar

Soya vinaigrette

2 egg yolks
1 tablespoon mustard
7 dl grapeseed oil, juice of 1 lime
2 dl sweet soya sauce
2 cloves of garlic

Scallop carpaccio

4 scallops

Avocado cream

3 avocados, 50 g mascarpone
10 basil leaves

Tuna

200 g tuna, a dash of olive oil
zest of 1 Chinese orange
(or lime, as an alternative)

PREPARATION

Marinated tuna

Allow the sugar to lightly caramelise, then douse with the balsamic vinegar. Add successively the lemon juice, coriander, ginger and garlic. Mix well and pass through a sieve. Add the soya sauce to the resulting liquid.
Steep the tuna block in this marinade and fry briefly on each of the four sides.
Cut the block into slices measuring ½ cm thick.

Soya vinaigrette

Process all the ingredients in a blender, until they form a vinaigrette. Keep to one side in a cool place for later.

Scallop carpaccio

Cut 4 scallops into fine, carpaccio-like slices and marinate them with olive oil and a little fleur de sel.

Avocado cream

Peel the avocados and mix them to a creamy consistency with the basil and the mascarpone, adding some salt, pepper and a little lemon juice.

Tuna

Cut the tuna into fine blocks and finish with some olive oil, sesame seeds, salt, pepper and the zest of a Chinese orange. Finish with some fresh herbs and dress as shown in the photograph.

Wout Bru is a passionate chef with a 'weakness' for fine flavours. His subtle cooking, with its harmonious balance between textures, colours and original presentation, is guaranteed to entice even the most discriminating food-lovers. He is constantly searching for new and magical food experiences, based on subtle yet daring combinations.

MORE
than just a hotel

....

BRASSERIE CHEZ BRU

Before their Provençal adventure, Wout and Suzy Bru worked in prominent restaurants in Flanders and London. In 1995 they went to Eygalières to convert an old village property into *'Le Bistrot d'Eygalières.'* Three years later Wout already had his first Michelin star. The front of the brasserie reminds one of a regular village café, but on the inside it is tastefully decorated. The cuisine is light and refined. The great success of the brasserie and the encouragement of guests such as Caroline of Monaco and Jean-Paul Belmondo persuaded Wout and Suzy to open a hotel as well which resulted in the just as successful 'Maison Bru.'

....

WORTH DISCOVERING

The wine estate 'Château Valdition

In the renaissance this estate was the property of no one less than King François I, who gave it to his daughter, Caroline du Prévot, for her marriage with the nobleman Ludovic Dacla de Châteaubert. For five centuries thereafter this estate remained in the possession of this family.

Along an impressive driveway you view several hectares of vineyards and olive groves. Both the white and the red South-French grape types are carefully grown biologically. The vines are pruned manually and the excess bunches of grapes are removed so the nutrition from the roots can be distributed over a limited number of grapes.

Next to the castle you find a shop where, in addition to the various kinds of olive oil, tapenades and other traditional culinary delicacies, you can also buy wine.

04

OUSTAU DE BAUMANIÈRE

In Le Val d'Enfer, where Dante found inspiration for his world-famous *Inferno*, Raymond Thuillier discovered a deserted farmhouse before the Second World War. He wanted to make it into a unique hotel with a gastronomic restaurant, but the war interrupted his plans.

He revived his plan in 1945 and the beau monde soon discovered this magic spot as they travelled from the chilly north to the Côte d'Azur. The atmosphere and the food that Raymond brought to his Ousteau de Baumanière was sufficient to persuade many wealthy travellers to postpone their trip to the coast for a few days. In the meantime, the innumerable important guests have put this remote Devil's Valley on the map, from Queen Elizabeth of England to Bono and Luciano Pavarotti.

No one less than Georges Pompidou, former president of France, described the new hotspot in 1969 in this way: *'Thanks to Raymond Thuillier, Les Beau, a godforsaken ghost village, has regained its joy of living. With his refined cuisine he has introduced there the elegant French lifestyle.'*

In the eighties Raymond Thuillier was joined by his grandson, Jean-André Charial, who had served as an apprentice with the greatest chefs of the country, such as Paul Bocuse, the Troisgros brothers and Alain Chapel. During the next twenty years, the L'Ousteau duo would create a consummate institute of refinement. At present, Thuillier only supervises in the kitchen and is responsible along with his wife, Geneviève, for quality control and reception of the guests.

Sylvestre Wahid, a practitioner of the cooking philosophy of Baumanière, allows himself to be guided by the traditions of the past, but always manages to give these timeless flavours a contemporary twist. To achieve this, he follows the seasons and his own inspiration of the moment.

WITH THE CHEF'S OWN TOUCH...

FOIE GRAS WITH VINEYARD PEACH

INGREDIENTS

1 kg foie gras (lobe)

Sangria jelly

1 litre red wine
½ litre water
300 g sugar
1 green apple
2 oranges
zest of 1 yellow lemon
1 bunch of blue grapes
6 g lavender
8 verbena leaves
8 grains of green cardamom
5 grains of long pepper
15 g agaragar

Vineyard peach marmalade

1 kg vineyard peaches
8 verbena leaves + 6 for finishing
8 grains of green cardamom
3 grains of white cardamom
300 g sugar
zest of 1 yellow lemon
8 leaves of purple basil
1 bunch of red grapes

Peach puree

1 litre white peach juice
50 g reduced vineyard peach syrup
9 g agaragar

PREPARATION

Sangria jelly

Pour the wine, water and sugar into a steel pan with straight edges. Bring this fluid to boiling point and then add first the herbs (lavender, green cardamom) and then the apple, the orange and the zest of lemon. Finally add the verbena leaves and then remove the pan from the heat. Cover and allow to stand for 20 minutes. Strain the sangria through a conical sieve, bring to the boil, add the agaragar and allow to boil for a further 3 minutes. Pour the resulting jelly onto a number of plates and keep in a cool place.

Vineyard peach marmalade

Peel the peaches. Place them in a vacuum bag, together with the herbs, lemon, verbena, basil, grapes and sugar. Cook for 45 minutes in a steam oven. When cooked and cooled, take the peaches out of the bag. Extract the stones from the peaches, and remove the cardamom, lemon zest, grapes and any pips from the bag. Mash the peach flesh with a fork. Place the flesh in a large pan on the edge of a low heat and cook further until a jam-like pulp results. Allow to cool. Add the finely-diced verbena leaves. Keep the fluid in which the peaches were cooked; this will be used for the puree for plate decoration.

Peach puree

Heat the juice of the white peaches and add the fluid in which the vineyard peaches were cooked. Bring to the boil, add the agaragar and boil for a further 3 minutes. Remove from the heat and keep in a cool place. As soon as the cooling is complete, mix the jelly in a Thermomix until it forms a smooth peach puree.

MORE
than just a hotel

LA PLACE

At the request of his customers, Jean-André Charial opened a charming bistro with a daily fresh, refined cuisine in the nearby village of Maussane-les-Alpilles. Behind the cooker stands the fourth generation, led by the friendly Marie-Noëlle Charial, daughter of Jean-André.

She learned the tricks of the trade in three-star restaurants such as '*La Maison de Bricourt*' in Cancale and '*Le Petit Nice*' in Marseille, and of course also in the restaurant of her father.

WORTH DISCOVERING

Carrières de Lumières

The massif of Les Alpilles, and in particular that of the Val d' Enfer, consists of limestone rocks. The now abandoned quarry is currently the decor for an impressive sound and light display. You can walk around in a labyrinth of metres' high caves in which images are projected 360 degrees and music is played. Each year this installation is built up around a different theme. Van Gogh and Gaugin, each with his own colour and painting style, are the subject of this unique art project.

05

LA CABRO D'OR

La Cabro d'Or gets its name from the poem *'Mireille'* by Frédéric Mistral that celebrates the love between a wealthy young lady and a poor goat herder.

Originally, La Cabro d'Or was conceived as the rural subsidiary of L'Oustau de Baumanière, but over the years the five-star hotel has firmly established its own identity. The hotel, located on an estate of two hectares, remains however the little brother of the legendary luxury hotel, Oustau de Baumanière.

This exclusive resort is located at the foot of the picturesque village, Les Baux-de-Provence, and is surrounded by the jagged limestone rock formations of the Val d'Enfer. The nearby riding stables, the goats and the ducks on the estate, as well as the biological vegetable garden, create a rural atmosphere. Yet the complex also has an atmosphere of refined luxury, thanks to the splendid swimming pool, the spa, the private pavements that overlook the gardens and the famous star restaurant.

WITH THE CHEF'S OWN TOUCH...

PLANCHA ROASTED SCALLOPS AND A SOFT AND CREAMY RISOTTO WITH SAFFRON AND HONEY FROM PROVENCE, ACCOMPANIED BY A VINAIGRETTE WITH THE JUICE OF CITRUS FRUITS

INGREDIENTS

For 8 people

48 fresh scallops

30 cl orange juice

4 oranges

24 stems of green asparagus from Provence

1 handful of chives

¼ handful of coriander

olive oil from the valley of Les Baux (quantity as preferred)

Risotto

600 g Carnarolli rice

2 white onions

12 g zest of orange

saffron stigmas (quantity as preferred)

1 ½ litres white poultry stock

120 g honey from Provence

fresh coriander (quantity as preferred)

PREPARATION

Grate the desired quantity of orange zest for the risotto recipe, then peel the oranges and remove the flesh. Keep in a cool place.

Allow the orange juice to reduce gradually and douse with some olive oil.

Prepare the asparagus. Boil them in salted water and then refresh in ice-cold water.

Sauté the finely diced onion in a pan and then colour the rice and orange zest, gradually adding the poultry stock. When the rice is cooked, add the honey and allow to cool in a dish.

Fry the scallops in an ungreased pan. Douse with olive oil and fresh butter. Turn the scallops over, remove them from the heat and dress the plates.

Shortly before serving, arrange the flesh of the oranges on the asparagus.

Michel Hulin's cuisine is renowned for its use of biologically-grown produce and Les Baux olive oil (AOC).

His cooking is exceptionally creative and always fresh. Olive oil flavours every dish on his menu, which is based in its entirety on local produce.

MORE
than just a hotel

SPA BAUMANIÈRE

In the *'Spa Baumanière'* exclusive use is made of the products of *'Une Olive en Provence'* based on the olive tree. This cosmetics brand was established by Annabel and Jean-Baptiste Quenin, a couple from Maussane-les-Alpilles. As the son of an olive oil producer, Jean-Baptiste knows all the secrets of the olive tree and that knowledge is incorporated in his products. Extracts from the blossoms of the olive tree have a relaxing effect. Extracts from the leaves have an anti-oxidant effect, while the concentrated oil of the plant purifies and hydrates the skin.

WORTH DISCOVERING

Le Vin à la Bouche

You can visit the most beautiful and interesting wine estates in the Provence under the expert guidance of an oenologist, who takes you along to the mythical estates where the various labels are produced. In the wine cellars you can often taste not only the wine, but also the local olive oil, cheeses and truffles. You can learn to taste wines on estates such as Châteauneuf du Pape, Gigondas, Vacquéras, Côtes du Rhône, Côtes de Luberon and Ventoux.

06

LODGE DE LA FOUQUE

Gérard Louvin is a well-known television personality in France. Before he launched himself in the hotel business, he was cook and maître d'hôtel for enterprises such as the *Companie des Wagons-Lits* and the prestigious *Orient-Express*. Six years ago, the opportunity to be patron of the Lodge de la Fouque was given to Louvin, born and raised in the Camargue, rather incidentally. It was a dream that became reality with the help of business partners, Daniel Moyne and Jean-Philippe Cartier. He completely renewed the four-star hotel, but retained the typical rural character.

You reach this magic spot, located in the nature park of the Camargue, two kilometres from Les-Saintes-Maries-de-la-Mer and its endless beaches, via a long driveway. Because the Lodge de la Fouque lies in a protected nature reserve, it must follow strict ecological guidelines, which simply strengthen the rural character.

The rooms, each with a unique interior design, are distributed among the lakes on the estate from where you can see the extraordinary fauna, pink flamingos, wild ducks, horses and bulls. In brief, this is the Camargue at its best!

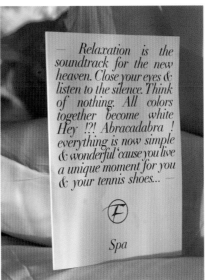

— Relaxation is the soundtrack for the new heaven. Close your eyes & listen to the silence. Think of nothing. All colors together become white. Hey !?! Abracadabra ! everything is now simple & wonderful 'cause you live a unique moment for you & your tennis shoes...

𝓕

Spa

WITH THE CHEF'S OWN TOUCH...

CAMARGUE BEEF WITH RED RICE

INGREDIENTS

For 4 people

1 kg Camargue (AOC) beef
(neck, cheeks)
2 stalks of thyme
1 laurel leaf
1 clove of garlic
2 red onions, large
zest of ½ grapefruit
3 carrots, large, with tops
2 dl olive oil
50 g olives from Les Baux
salt and pepper
1 bottle of red wine (Costières
de Nîmes or Côtes du Rhône
Gardoises)

320 g biologically-grown red
rice from Camargue (AOC)
1 laurel leaf
1 clove of garlic
1 onion
2 carrots
¼ bunch of spring onions
10 g fleur de sel
1 cl olive oil from Les Baux (AOC)

PREPARATION

Cut the meat into pieces and marinate it for 24 hours in the red wine, together with the finely chopped onion, sliced carrots, orange zest, thyme, garlic and laurel.
Heat the olive oil in a frying pan. Drain the pieces of meat and coat them finely with flour. Brown the meat pieces in the pan. Remove and place in a casserole dish.
Pass the marinade through a conical sieve and add the resulting fluid to the meat until it is fully covered.
Stew for 4 hours on a very low heat.
As the end of the cooking time approaches, check the consistency of the sauce. This must be thick and syrupy.
When this stage is reached, add the olives and season according to preference before serving.
Serve on a plate or in a small casserole pot.
Allow the rice to soak in sufficient water overnight.
Drain and pat dry.
Make a vegetable stock using a finely chopped onion, two sliced carrots, a clove of garlic and a laurel leaf.
When the stock reaches boiling point, add the rice.
Allow to cook for 25 to 30 minutes, making sure that the grains of rice open gradually and do not burst.
Finely dice the spring onions.
Allow the cooked rice to drain, season with fleur de sel, and dress with a little olive oil and the diced spring onion.
Serve in a dish or in a small heat-retaining pot.

Chef Frédérick Pelletier, a French-speaking Canadian, is passionate about the Camargue and has been inspired by its charm.
For the Mas de la Fouque he has put together a menu card focused on the region's many delicious local products: red rice, black rice, wild shrimps, beef from biological-reared cattle with quality labels, but also potatoes and sand carrots.

MORE
than just a hotel

....

LE PARC ORNITHOLOGIQUE

This park, known for its pink flamingos, is located in the middle of an expansive nature reserve where the Lodge de la Fouque is also located. You can explore the gigantic estate by means of the kilometres-long walking paths through the marshes and among the pools. Information panels give information about the fauna and flora of the Camargue. In special *volières* injured birds are cared for. The park is an initiative of an involved resident of the Camargue, André Lamouroux.

....

La nutrition

La coloration du plumage n'est pas l'apanage d'un sexe, ni d'une saison que l'on rencontre aussi bien en hiver été des flamants très colorés. A la ce le poussin est recouvert d'un duvet n bec est droit et rose, tout comme Au bout d'une semaine le duvet s foncé, le bec et les pattes oirs. Il restera ainsi jusqu'à

e progressivement jusqu'à nuancé de gris, blanc et 1 an et demi, pour le sa parure adulte où et 7 ans. Il est alors

e, il se nourrit uatiques, de is consom- s plantes

ngère sco-

Pourquoi les flamants sont roses ?

Camargue marquage plus grand mant est éq tique sur la lisible au télé pour ne pas dé

Son mode de
mières

Les 15 000 oiseau

WORTH DISCOVERING

The gypsies and their celebration

From the Lodge da la Fouque you notice on the horizon, behind the gleaming pools of water with bathing birds, the contours of Saintes-Maries-de-la-Mer. This snow-white village is especially known for its church that also served as a fort during the attacks of the Saracens, for its typical huts with straw roofs, its dunes with endless beaches and for its gypsies.

Each year on 24 May gypsies from the whole world gather here to celebrate the feast of their patron saint, Sara. This mythical personage has never been recognised as a saint by the Catholic Church, but that does not prevent the gypsy community from coming here on a pilgrimage and organising a gigantic celebration in which large fires are lit and the image of the saint is carried to the beach.

07

LE MAS DE PEINT

The subsoil of the Rhône in the delta area near Arles is somewhat salty. Here and there, pools and ponds develop with brackish water. The ground is fertile enough to graze horses and bulls and to grow rice.

It is therefore a surprise in the midst of this rugged environment, in the unsightly hamlet of Le Sambuc, to find Le Mas de Peint, a seventeenth-century farmhouse in white stone on an estate of five-hundred hectares.

The farmhouse was built for a certain Antoine Peint, but for generations now it has been in the possession of the Bon family. In the nineties, Lucille Bon, the wife of the late Jacques Bon, decided to make their magnificent family estate available for guests. Lucille is an architect and turned the impressive farmhouse into a place of light, space and elegance without compromising the authenticity of the complex.

Everything in the hotel is typically Camargue with antique furniture from the region, old photos of bull fights and of the *manade* with its *gardians* on their horses. You imagine that you are home in the cosy salon and the pleasant restaurant in the kitchen.

Le Mas de Peint has twelve rooms, each of which is finished off in every detail. Lucille Bon still runs the hotel, while her son, Frédéric, operates the adjacent *manade*, a breeding farm for bulls and horses.

WITH THE CHEF'S OWN TOUCH...

FRESH BRETON LOBSTER WITH A TAGLIATELLE OF MULTI-COLOURED CARROT, SERVED WITH A RASPBERRY VINAIGRETTE

INGREDIENTS

For 4 persons

4 blue lobsters
1 yellow carrot
1 orange carrot
1 purple carrot
2 aubergines
raspberry vinegar
olive oil from Camargue (AOC)
salt and pepper

For the raspberry vinaigrette

3 tablespoons olive oil
1 tablespoon raspberry vinegar
1 tablespoon Dijon mustard
2 finely diced cloves of garlic
1 pinch of thyme
salt and freshly-ground pepper

PREPARATION

Cook the aubergines for 25 minutes in the oven at 190 °C, following which they can be finely diced with a knife to create an aubergine caviar.

Cook the blue lobsters for 9 minutes in a large pot of boiling water. When cooked, remove the lobsters from their shells and keep in a cool place.

Cut the different carrots into fine strips and cook them for 2 minutes in boiling water.

Carefully stir together all the ingredients for the raspberry vinaigrette.

Dress on a plate according to your own preferences.

Vincent Laisney was born in Normandy, where he learnt the art of fine cooking.

He eventually moved to Paris, where he first worked in the Atelier de Joël Robuchon and later in La Grande Cascade.

In 2008 Vincent became a kitchen assistant at Mas de Peint and was appointed as chef in 2011.

His gastronomic Mediterranean cuisine is based primarily on fresh regional produce.

He prepares a new menu each day, depending on what the market has to offer.

MORE
than just a hotel

A DAY AT THE MANADE

This unique experience allows you to spend a day at the manade. First you are welcomed by the gardians at the '*Cabano dis Ego*,' the ranch of Le Mas de Peint. Then you see how they brand a young bull and you are introduced to the '*jeux de gardians*' and the gardians show how they ride a Camargue horse. In the '*jeux de bouquet*' a girl chooses her horseman. As a noonday meal you eat a grilled beefsteak. In the afternoon a '*course à la cocarde*' takes place where the bulls are decorated with a ribbon and then let loose in the arena of the '*Cabano dis Ego*.' The gardian challenges the bull until he attacks. The idea is to grab the ribbon and jump over the fence as fast as possible to escape the horns of the bull.

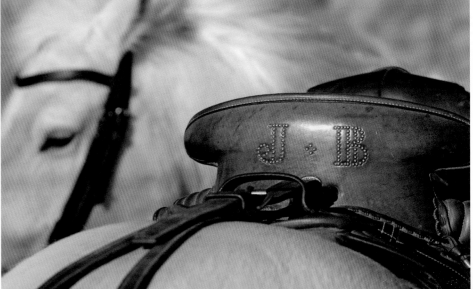

WORTH DISCOVERING

The Camargue

You can explore the estate around Le Mas de Peint and the whole Camargue on foot, by horse, by bicycle or with a 4x4. Just beyond the hotel you find the 'Domaine de Palissade,' a walking area of seven-hundred hectares, located on the Grand-Rhône, and strewn with pools of water. If you go farther toward the sea, you gradually leave the green meadows with bulls and horses behind you, and after the many pools and lakes you reach the dunes and the kilometres-long beaches. Here you find colourful caravans and buses, left behind by hippies who secluded themselves here in the sixties to live it up, far removed from civilisation. The government wants to clean up the place, but there is resistance from action groups wanting to keep the spot intact. In any case, the mythical atmosphere that hangs around these dunes will never disappear.

08

VILLA GALLICI

Hidden among the green heights of Aix-en-Provence, and a five-minute walk from the Cours Mirabeau with its
centuries old plane trees, we find this small pearl. The charming hotel combines the typical Provençal style with an
Italian accent.

The light of Cézanne shines in the Florentine garden and the shadow of the cypresses is reflected in the swimming
pool. During the last two centuries the wind and the sun have given the outside walls a beautiful honey colour.

It is almost unbelievable that this bastide, bathed in the aroma of laurel and lavender, was still desolate and overrun
by weeds at the beginning of the nineties.

Three friends, Daniel Jouve, Gil Dez and Charles Montemarco, were able to convert the estate into a place of rest and
refinement. The pale yellow colour of the outside walls is carried over into the interior, which subtly emphasises the
antique furniture and paintings. Exceptional are the curtains in the salons and the rooms, that are the work of great
designers such as Canovas, Frey and Nobilis.

The Villa Gallici abundantly meets the conditions of Relais & Châteaux for its members. It is a magnificent bastide,
a fortress that breathes the typical character of the region. It possesses French refinement relative to interior design,
service and gastronomy.

WITH THE CHEF'S OWN TOUCH...

VELOUTÉ OF BOLETUS MUSHROOMS WITH NUT OIL AND FRESH TRUFFLE, SERVED WITH A TARRAGON-SPICED BOLETUS BRUNOISE AND A FRIED QUAIL'S EGG

INGREDIENTS

For 4 people

400 g fresh boletus mushrooms (200g + 200g)

2 shallots

8 cl nut oil

10 g fresh truffle

4 quail's eggs

2 slices of white bread

300 g white poultry stock

15 cl liquid cream

5 cl white wine

20 g butter

salt and pepper

olive oil and fresh herbs for dressing

PREPARATION

Clean the mushrooms and cut half of them into rough cubes. Cut the remaining half into a brunoise and keep in a cool place. Sauté a diced shallot in 10 g of butter with a dash of olive oil. Add the roughly chopped mushrooms, season with pepper and salt and allow to stew on a high heat. Douse with the poultry stock and 100 g of liquid cream. Allow to simmer for 45 minutes, then mix thoroughly and pass through a conical sieve. Season according to preference and keep warm.

Finely dice the remaining shallot and sauté it in 10 g of butter with a dash of olive oil. Douse with the white wine and allow to reduce. Add the boletus brunoise, season with pepper and allow to stew gently for 15 minutes, stirring regularly.

Using a ring with a diameter of 3 cm, cut a number of roundels out of the slices of white bread. Toast them on both sides and keep them at room temperature.

Fry the quail's eggs in a pan. When ready, cut them to the same size and shape as the toasted circlets. Keep warm.

Arrange the boletus brunoise in the centre of a plate and place a toasted circlet on top. Pour the warm velouté around this composition. Grate some fresh truffle over the plate, finish with a little nut oil and decorate with fresh herbs.

Chef Christophe Gavot learnt his craft at the hotel school in Monaco and is well-known for his refined cooking with a distinctive hint of the Provence. He follows the seasons and is keen to play the 'quality-product' card, whilst still respecting time-honoured methods of preparation.

In Villa Gallici subtly balanced tastes and centuries-old traditions go hand in hand with exoticism and the very latest culinary trends.

MORE
than just a hotel

....

VIP TREATMENT

The personal service of Villa Gallici is exceptionally exclusive and refined. On arrival the guest are offered an ice-cold *Dé Maison* with almond cake and fruit in season. At noon you can enjoy a broad assortment of teas with daily-fresh bakery goods.

....

WORTH DISCOVERING

In the footsteps of Cézanne

The atelier of Cézanne is located a stone's throw from the Villa
Gallici. Thus, you can very easily visit from there all the places
where the painter produced the largest portion of his works.
The city of Aix has mapped out a route that starts with a visit to the
atelier of Cézanne and then to the family estate, *'Jas de Bouffan.'*
The next stop is at Mont Sainte-Victoire, the mountain that
Cézanne painted dozens of times, sometimes even several times
in one day, to capture the various lighting effects on canvas.
The route ends back at Aix, for a walk along the Cours Mirabeau
and the brasserie *'Les Deux Garçons,'* where the painter was
a regular customer.

09

HOSTELLERIE DE L'ABBAYE DE LA CELLE

This twelfth-century abbey, in the midst of the vineyards of the Coteaux Varois in the small village of Celle now emits an impressive calm. That was different in the past. On the sly, the Benedictines served as ladies of the night, a secret that they were able to hide from the outside world behind the thick walls of the abbey.

After this scandal came to light, the abbey remained vacant for centuries until Alain Ducasse discovered the estate in 1999 and transformed it into a high-class luxury hotel.

The restaurant consists of three splendid salons. A pavement overlooks a magnificent park with cypresses, a vegetable garden and a vineyard. Irrigation is done by two natural springs that also supply water for the fountains. The vegetable garden has dozens of types of tomatoes, basil and courgettes in addition to other herbs such as pepper and fennel.

Past the swimming pool, built on the remains of a Roman villa, you enter a garden with fruit trees and berry bushes reaching to the former beguinage. The old chapel currently houses a boutique with regional products such as wine, honey, olive oil and cookbooks by Alain Ducasse.

Benoît Witz was one of the first followers of Alain Ducasse. He received his training at Ducasse's Louis XV restaurant in Monaco and has remained faithful to the culinary philosophy of his great teacher. It is no coincidence that this hostelry is a favourite meeting place of the region's gourmets and gastronomes. His success is built on pure products, professional expertise and his own inspirational ideas.

WITH THE CHEF'S OWN TOUCH...

SAND CAKE WITH BOLETUS MUSHROOMS AND LOBSTER TAILS IN BASIL

INGREDIENTS

For 4 people

Sand pastry mix

125 g flour

80 g butter

25 g water

20 g egg

2.5 g salt

5 g sugar

1 handful of common green basil

1 handful of opal basil

1 handful of fennel

1 handful of thyme (or 3 stalks)

20 lobster tails

12 white borage flowers

1 white onion

5 shallots

600 g boletus mushrooms

40 g almond powder

8 cl white balsamic vinegar

15 cl oil from ripe olives

10 cl lobster juice

a dash of cognac

fine-grained salt

fleur de sel and freshly-ground pepper

PREPARATION

Sand pastry

Spread the pastry out flat and cut it into four slices of 11 cm. Bake for 12 minutes in an oven at 160°C. Turn off the heat and allow to rest in the oven for a further 5 minutes.

Clean the boletus mushrooms. Remove the stems and cut them into cubes. Cut the caps into thin slices.

Boletus paste

Dice the onion and sauté it with 80 g of the finely chopped boletus cubes. Douse with the vinegar and allow to cook in a covered pot for 10 minutes. Add the almond powder. Mix with 6 cl of olive oil.

Clean the lobsters and remove the heads.
Place the tails in a pan and fry in hot olive oil with a little thyme and garlic. Douse with the cognac, cover with a lid and simmer for 3 minutes.
Peel the warm lobsters. Dice the shallot and allow it to simmer for 8 to 10 minutes with the boletus brunoise.

Make a reduced sauce with the lobster heads. Use a masher to crush them finely and then fry them in a cast-iron pan. Add the aromatic garnish (basil and fennel). Sauté briefly, then douse and dilute with water.
Allow to cook for a further 25 minutes and then pass through a sieve. If necessary, allow to simmer further until the fluid becomes syrupy.

Arrange the finely sliced boletus caps in a 10 cm ring and cover with the brunoise. Place a slice of sand pastry on top and heat in the oven for 5 minutes at 180 °C. Turn out onto a grille.

Presentation

Decorate the edge of the plate with three drops of boletus paste and the boletus mushrooms. Add another drop of the salve to the centre of the plate. This will fix the cake in place.
Decorate with the basil leaves and the lobster tails. Season with salt and pepper.
Finish with the borage flowers and serve with a splash of juice.

MORE
than just a hotel

LA MAISON DES VINS COTEAUX VAROIS

In an old chapel on the inner court of the abbey you
find a shop with regional products such as aromatic
honey, rice for risotto, olive oil and herbs. Right next
to it is the wine tasting annex of the wine shop
'La Maison des Coteaux Varois de Provence.' Eighty wine
estates from the Var are represented, including the
wines of the estate L' Abbaye de la Celle itself

WORTH DISCOVERING

On our way to visit the houses of Ducasse

This two-day trip, mapped out by Alain Ducasse, leads the traveller north from his abbey in Celle in the green Var region, to his 'bastide' in Moustiers-Sainte-Marie in the Alpes de Haute-Provence. You ride along the massif of Sainte-Baume where Maria Magdalena is said to have gone after the death of Christ to live as a recluse, to the prehistoric cave dwellings of Cotignac and the Abbey of Thoronet. Via Tourtour or the so-called 'village at the gate of heaven,' Aups, known for its truffle market, and Lac Sainte-Croix, you arrive at your final destination, Moustiers-Sainte-Marie, the central city of the faience.

10

CHÂTEAU DE BERNE

At the end of a long road through the Maquis, near Lorgues and Flayosc in the Var region, vineyards and olive groves suddenly rise up from nowhere. Along a stately cypress-lined drive you come to a castle that is reminiscent of a Tuscan *castello*. Beside it is a large, white bastide: Château de Berne.

The estate lies on the *Via Aurelia*, a Roman road that connected Italy with Spain and was used mainly for wine transport. This drink of the gods was already being produced in the region two-thousand years ago. Bearing witness of this are the ruins of a Roman villa where amphora were found (two-handled jars with a narrow neck) that served for stocking, transporting and preserving wine.

From the sun-rich rooms and suites you have a view of the many vineyards and olive groves. In Château de Berne room numbers are not used but names such as 'La Chambre Lavande' or 'La Chambre Olivier.'

The estate of almost five-hundred hectares rightly belongs to the prestigious Relais & Châteaux chain and is a perfect combination of the art of running a hotel and the art of producing wine.

WITH THE CHEF'S OWN TOUCH...
DUCK FOIE GRAS WITH A CARROT AND GRAPEFRUIT SAUCE

INGREDIENTS

For 4 people
250 g terrine of foie gras
1 litre carrot juice
10 small tricholoma mushrooms
juice of 1 grapefruit
10 leaves of rocket salad
(rucola)
50 g ginger
balsamic cream
(quantity as preferred)
Suze (a liqueur based on
gentian; quantity as preferred)
sherry vinegar
(quantity as preferred)
2 slices of gelatine
a pinch of fleur de sel
some wild carrot flowers
salt and pepper

PREPARATION

Heat the carrot juice with small cubes of diced ginger and allow to reduce on a low heat.
Add the grapefruit juice and allow to reduce still further. When the liquid becomes syrupy, add the Suze, vinegar and gelatine. Season with salt and pepper.
Cut the foie gras into four roundels, using a small metal ring. Brush two of the roundels with the reduced carrot juice mixture.
Wash the mushrooms, season with salt and place them for 1 minute under the salamander.

Arrange on plate.
Brush a stripe of the reduced carrot juice onto the plate. Make a tower with two roundels of foie gras, the rocket salad and the mushrooms. Finish with a little fleur de sel and the wild carrot flowers.

Sébastien Nouveau likes to do things differently. His instinctive cooking is a delight for any palate. One of the most important values of this chef is his respect for his products. He takes great pleasure in incorporating the delights of his own kitchen garden into his refined cuisine: edible flowers, aromatic plants, forgotten vegetables, fruit from his orchard... For all his dishes — starters, main courses and desserts — he always uses seasonal products, bursting with colour and flavour.

MORE
than just a hotel

THE WINE ESTATE

The estate forms an oasis of five-hundred hectares in the midst of endless forests and the Maquis. A forth of the area has been planted in vineyards with grape types that grow well in the warm climate, the rest consists of olive groves. For fifteen years ecological principles have been applied by using a minimum of chemical pesticides and herbicides. Château de Berne has been given the label *'Agriculture raisonnée.'*
The wine estate goes even farther in its ecological commitment. The young wines are now sold, mostly in warm holiday areas, in completely recyclable PET bottles.

WORTH DISCOVERING
Lorgues

As already mentioned, the history of Château de Berne and of the magnificent Provençal city of Lorgues goes back two-thousand years. The name Lorgues derives from the Latin *'lonicus,'* and refers to the central location of the Mediaeval village. You can walk for hours along the route that the city has lined out for visitors, which runs along the many fountains, squares and narrow alleys. Going via the Rue de l'Eglise you come to the Collégiale Saint-Martin, the eighteenth-century church in white stone.

VILLA MARIE

The peninsula of Saint-Tropez is unbelievably beautiful. Small sand pathways wind along magnificent estates hiding among the Maquis and the vineyards or beside deserted beaches, creeks and bays. Not to be missed are the picturesque villages of Gassin and Ramatuelle, nestled high on top of the hills like two cherries on a tart.
Villa Marie is located on the Route des Plages in the midst of all of this natural beauty with a breath-taking view of the bay of Pampelonne. The Provençal villa towers above an immense park of conifers, parasol pines and palm trees. The owners are Jocelyne and Jean-Louis Sibuèt, an industrious couple who also have several other beautiful hotels in Megève in the Alps, in the Luberon and in Lyon.
The lady of the house has completely renovated and redecorated the hotel, but was able to retain the authentic atmosphere of the original villa. Jean-Louis in turn was able to express himself completely in the park of three hectares that he has divided into seven thematic gardens including fountains and a swimming pool with rock masses.
Each space has its own distinctive atmosphere, from the veranda with beautiful flowers to the bar with its exceptional shell decorations. Here, however, most of your time is spent outside. On one of the many pavements, surrounded by luscious gardens, you can have breakfast, lunch or dinner and enjoy a delicious gastronomic meal.

WITH THE CHEF'S OWN TOUCH...

SKIN-FRIED JOHN DORY, WITH CANDIED FENNEL AND AN ORANGE SAUCE

INGREDIENTS

For 4 people
2 John Dory's, weighing approximately 600 g each (filets)
8 g fennel
3 litres orange juice
200 g squid
120 g purple garlic
100 g olive oil
40 g candied tomatoes
Espelette pepper
4 sprigs talks of thyme
4 sprigs of rosemary
20 g Camargue salt
pepper

PREPARATION

Peel the fennel, cut it in two and blanch it in boiling salted water. Place both halves in a dish and cover completely with orange juice. Seal the dish with grease-free paper and cook for 30 minutes in an oven at 180 °C. Reduce the temperature to 110 °C and cook for a further 1½ hours. Drain and keep to one side for later.

Wash the John Dory filets and keep them in a cool place. Finely dice two onions and sauté them in a little olive oil. Crush the extracted fish bones as finely as possible and add them to the onion. Cover with 1½ litres of orange juice and allow to simmer for 20 minutes. Pass the mixture through a conical sieve and allow to reduce on a low heat until the juice becomes syrupy.

Cut the squid into strips measuring 5 cm long and 5 mm wide. Keep in a cool place. Lightly colour the fennel on both sides in a warm pan with a little olive oil. Season according to preference. Season the fish fillets on both sides with salt, pepper and Espelette pepper. Fry the fillets lightly in a pan, starting with the skin side. When the skin is sufficiently crisp, turn the fillets over. Cook for a further 8 minutes in an oven at 180 °C. Braise the slices of squid in olive oil. Season with salt from the Camargue, pepper and Espelette pepper. Add the candied tomatoes.

Presentation

Neatly arrange the half fennel, the fillets of John Dory and the squid strips on an oval plate. Pour the orange sauce generously over the fennel and the fish. Dress the squid with a light brushing of olive oil and season with a twist of the pepper mill. Decorate before serving with the sprigs of thyme and rosemary. Sprinkle with a little of the Camargue salt.

Chef Lionel Arnoux of Villa Marie opts resolutely for delicious ingredients from the south and takes us on a sunny voyage of discovery through a wide range of tasty regional products. A dash of creativity, seasoned with a touch of finesse and finished with a sprinkling of passion: the perfect recipe for a rich and inventive menu.

MORE
than just a hotel

....

PURE ALTITUDE

The hotel spa works with 'Pure Altitude' products,
a brand of beauty and wellness products developed by
the owner of Villa Marie, Jocelyne Sibuèt. In the
French Alps, more specifically in Megève, the Sibuèts
operate several luxury hotels that have a spa. The medicinal herbs and plants present in the Alps inspired
Jocelyne to create her own range of care products and
cosmetics that originally were only used and sold in
her own hotels. Because of its great success, however,
the range is now sold world-wide under the name
'Pure Altitude,' a name that refers to the purity of the
mountains, the air and the water.

....

WORTH DISCOVERING

Château Minuty

This wine estate replaced grape types such as *carignan* and *ugni blanc* with authentic Provençal types in order to produce exclusively superior wines.

The white wine is *made* on the basis of the *rolle*, a typical grape in the Var, the red on the basis of *syrah* and *mourvèdre*, and finally the rosé on the basis of *grenache* and *tibouren*. The vineyards face the Gulf of Saint-Tropez to the southwest and therefore get the right amount of sunlight. Furthermore, the gentle sea climate provides an ideal environment: after the blossoming time in the spring, the sea wind dries up the vines so the chance of mould and other diseases is less.

12

LA RÉSERVE DE RAMATUELLE

Where you hear only the sound of the sea and where Cap Taillat and the Mediterranean Sea form the horizon, that is where you find this exceptional hotel.

The building from the seventies underwent a metamorphosis thanks to hotel patron and architect Jean-Michel Wilmotte. The pure lines from Japanese architecture form a splendid contrast with the natural greenery and the bright blue sea. The rooms are housed in white, sand and ochre-coloured buildings. Each room has its own garden or pavement and a breath-taking view of the sea. Discrete luxury and privacy prevail.

All together, the estate has nine rooms designed by Jean-Michel Wilmotte, and twelve villas decorated by interior decorator Rémi Tessier, each with its own swimming pool and garden.

The spa continues the minimalistic Zen-style and forms a separate universe where each customer receives individualised treatment. You can relax in one of the eleven treatment cabins or have a dip in the twelve metre long indoor swimming pool or in the thirty metre long overflow swimming pool.

The view of the Mediterranean Sea is interrupted only by the small Cap Taillat peninsula, a protected nature reserve connected to the mainland only by a thirty metre long strip of sand. You seem to be at the very end of the world, although one of the most fashionable bathing cities in the world is only a stone's throw away.

WITH THE CHEF'S OWN TOUCH...

FILET OF LACQUERED LAMB WITH SOYA AND LEMON, ACCOMPANIED BY A TRUFFLE PUREE WITH OLIVE OIL

INGREDIENTS

For 4 people

2 lamb breasts

8 lamb ribs

40 g truffle pieces

20 g lemon honey

30 g rice vinegar

30 g soya sauce

zest of 1 lemon

50 g orange juice

20 g green lemon

100 g lamb juice

4 mini-carrots

4 mini-turnips

4 asparagus tips

4 cherry tomatoes

400 g Charlotte potatoes

olive oil

(extra virgin of good quality)

salt and pepper (quantity as preferred)

PREPARATION

Remove the fat from the lamb breasts, so that only the medallions of meat remain. Scrape away the ribs (one per person). Cut the filets in two lengthways. Keep in a cool place.

Marinade

Caramelise the honey and douse with the vinegar. Remove from the heat and allow to reduce briefly, before adding the soya sauce and the lemon zest. Marinate the meat.

Sauce with citrus fruits

Reduce the juice of the orange and lemon by half, add the lamb juice and reduce further until only a small residue remains. Check the seasoning. Keep to one side for later.

Vegetable garnish

Boil the vegetables in salted water and glaze once cooked. Season the tomatoes with salt and a little olive oil, then roast them in the oven. Peel the potatoes and boil them in salted water. When cooked, pour off the water and puree the potatoes immediately, without allowing them to cool. Add seasoning, a little olive oil and the truffle pieces. Stir carefully and keep warm in a bain-marie. Cook the filets a la plancha. Lacquer them with the soya and honey marinade and roast for just 2 minutes in an oven at 180 °C. Allow to rest for 1 minute and then brush clean.

Dress the truffle puree in a mould and decorate with alternating pieces of halved carrots, halved turnips, tomatoes and asparagus tips. Remove the mould, insert a rib into the puree and place the filet in a parallel position. Finish with a dash of sauce.

Éric Canino, previously a chef at Michel Guérard's restaurant in Gréoux-les-Bains and now running the kitchen at La Réserve de Ramatuelle, will be delighted to acquaint you with what he calls his 'wellness' cooking. His southern-based cuisine is bursting with Mediterranean flavour and the ingredients — chosen with great care — are always of the very highest quality.

It is clear that this chef has a preference for light recipes full of taste.

MORE
than just a hotel

....

UN PALACE

Some five-star hotels earn extra recognition because of their exceptional location, their aesthetic character, their architecture, gastronomy, service or background. For this reason the French government has appointed independent hotel authorities to select a handful of hotels that meet these extra conditions. These special hotels were given a separate classification of '*Palace*.' La Réserve de Ramatuelle has earned this exclusive recognition.

....

WORTH DISCOVERING

Nordic Walking in Saint-Tropez

For groups of at least four people, the hotel organises five day tours of fifteen to twenty kilometres of *Nordic walking* in the mountains of the Saint-Tropez peninsula. The programme is under the supervision of a medical doctor and starts each day with an hour of yoga before breakfast. After the physical effort, the participants are expected in the spa of La Réserve for a pleasant massage. The day is closed with a healthful Mediterranean meal.

13

PAN DEÏ PALAIS

Once upon a time there was a French general who fell hopelessly in love with a princes in the kingdom of Punjab. Jean-François Allard, a colonial from Saint-Tropez, imprisoned princes Bannu Pan Deï during a battle, but was himself conquered by her charms. In 1835 he took her with him back to France and had a magnificent palace built in the Rue Gambetta in Saint-Tropez. The villa was built completely in Indian style to make his bride feel at home. They had five children and lived happily ever after.

Hotel owner Stéphane Courbit was intrigued by this magic spot and purchased the premises in 2004. The building was restored to its former glory and the hotel joined the prestigious Relais & Châteaux chain. Once you walk through the wooden entrance gateway, you find yourself in a fairy-tale world of a thousand-and-one-nights.

The interior is dominated by red and ochre tints, and you find antique wooden panelling, eastern objects of art, and in the restaurant there are of course portraits of the general and his princes. The hall looks out on an attractive inner garden where you can nestle in luxurious garden furniture under a canopy, or have a dip in the swimming pool, decorated with mosaics.

Nothing causes you to suspect that beyond the hotel walls are found the luxury boutiques and the hustle and bustle of the Place des Lices.

WITH THE CHEF'S OWN TOUCH...

GILTHEAD STEAMED IN BANANA LEAVES

INGREDIENTS

For 4 people

2 giltheads (bream),
weighing 600 to 800 g

1 fresh banana leaf (edible)

Filling

800 g coconut cream

2 shallots

½ clump of chives

Espelette pepper
(quantity as preferred)

2 tablespoons honey

ginger (quantity as preferred)

salt and white pepper
(quantity as preferred)

PREPARATION

Wash and scale the giltheads. Remove the bones and skin.
Cut the filets into large pieces.
Prepare the filling by carefully stirring all the ingredients
into a homogenous mass.
Add the pieces of fish, mingle together thoroughly and
allow to rest for 20 minutes in a cool place.
Cut the banana leaf into squares measuring 20 cm by
20 cm. Place them flat on a work surface and add
a portion of fish and filling to one side of each leaf.
Roll up the leaves and check the edges. Fasten them
with a wooden toothpick.
Allow the rolls to rest in a cool place before cooking.
Make a steam basket. When ready, cover the fish rolls and
steam-cook them for 10 minutes.

Precision, purity, style...

*The refined cuisine of Renaud
Capelle, chef at the Pan dei Palais,
is as perfect as a Japanese garden
and as serene as the Land of the
Rising Sun itself.*

In a single word: zen.

MORE
than just a hotel

....

THE LOUNGE BAR

This hip lounge bar is the ideal starting point for a typical '*nuit tropézienne*.' The evening begins with soft lounge music but a few hours later the speakers are sending out festive dance music. You can taste the most delectable cocktails and wines from all parts of the world. Chef Renaud Capelle serves delicious amuse-bouches according to the season such as nehms, tapas and Serrano ham.

....

WORTH DISCOVERING

Petanque

Around the corner from the Pan deï Palais we find the famous
Place des Lices, the mecca of petanque. For centuries the best
players of France and from far beyond competed with each other
under the plane trees while engaging in animated discussions.
Each café on the square possesses with much pride the personal
ball sets of the best players of the past.

Petanque comes from the Provençal word *pétanco*, a combination
of *pé* (foot) and *tanco* (support post), and means 'feet positioned
so they stand firm as a post.'

14

SEZZ

Shahé Kalaidjian, an Armenian from Beirut who was raised in London, is a world-traveller and an atypical hotel owner. Five years after the opening of his hotel Sezz in Paris he sought a new challenge in the south. There he discovered another Saint-Tropez, away from all the glitter and glamour, where discrete luxury and privacy prevailed.
He noticed an old hotel for sale on the Plage de Salins. The complex was given luxuriant, subtropical greenery.
The thirty-five rooms were conceived of as separate houses around an immense swimming pool and the two suites are complete villas, each with a private swimming pool and pavement.
The famous designer Christophe Pillet was responsible for the interior design and drew his inspiration from the fifties, but with a contemporary look. In addition he wanted to carry the vacation and beach atmosphere over into both the rooms and the public areas such as the spa and the restaurant. Pillet works with pure lines, fresh colours and much light, by which he accomplished his mission without difficulty.
The restaurant is named after the writer Colette and relates to the relaxed and luxurious life in Saint-Tropez.
The Provençal pavement with olive trees and palm trees, and the glorious swimming pool make it complete.

MORE
than just a hotel

SPA PAYOT

Nadia Payot, a female medical doctor from the beginning of the last century, was passionately dedicated to the struggle against physical ageing. She based her beauty philosophy on exercise gymnastics for the face and good care products. In the spa of Hotel Sezz, all body and facial treatments are applied according to the *'modelage 42 mouvements'* of Payot, forty-two movements that revitalise the soul, improve beauty and restore the balance between mind and body.

WORTH DISCOVERING

Walking on the Plage des Canebiers

Hotel Sezz is located within walking distance from the unspoilt beach of Canebiers, far removed from all the pressures of life. A coastal pathway runs right and left from the beach to the end of the Saint-Tropez peninsula or to the city and the harbour itself. Whether you go past the splendid gardens and the villas on the way to the city centre or take the walk to the Cap, the view is breath-taking.

15

MUSE

Muse Ramatuelle is a tribute to the original muses, the daughters of Zeus with Mnemosyne, the goddess of memory. Muse is thus certainly not just one in a long line of luxury hotels. Here you have an exclusive view of the bay of Pampelonne and you can walk in the exceptional garden, designed by garden architect, Sophie Agata Ambroise, and planted according to ecological principles. The plants are irrigated, for example, by means of a waterfall.

The swimming pool with bright blue water also appears very natural; it looks like a tropical beach where the deck chairs stand with their feet almost in the water. Around the swimming pool stand four trim and stylish *cabanas* with beach chairs and curtains in front if you want to protect yourself from the sun. You can even enjoy lunch or dinner there in complete privacy.

The rooms, each with its own garden and some even with their own swimming pool, are conceived as private residences and have their own little wine cellar that can be filled according to the wishes of the customer.

The interior is mainly in light tints and is based on art-deco style.

MORE
than just a hotel

LA PISCINE

The idea of adding a breath-taking swimming pool to hotel Muse developed because the legendary film '*La Piscine*' with Romy Schneider and Alain Delon was filmed in the area. The overflow swimming pool forms the beating heart of the hotel. The exclusive character of the swimming pool is emphasised by the elegant gardens designed by Sophie Agata Ambroise, each of which is equipped with an advanced irrigation system.

WORTH DISCOVERING

Exploring the area by bicycle

Hotel Muse makes bicycles available to its guests free of charge
so they can explore the peninsula. The beaches of Pampelonne
and Canebiers are within 15 minutes cycling and the villages of
Ramatuelle, Gassin and Port Grimaud - also known as little Venice
- are not much farther. The lively Saint-Tropez with its exclusive
harbour is reached by bicycle even sooner. On the way you will
enjoy the Maquis, the vineyards and the magnificent villas hidden
among the greenery.

16

LA BASTIDE DE CAPELONGUE

Located at the top of the hills of the Provençal village of Bonnieux in the heart of Luberon, this estate enjoys a magnificent panorama of the largest cedar forest in Europe. The spread-out and luxurious charm hotel is a respected member of the Relais & Châteaux chain.

Actually it is a complex, subdivided into three hotels. *La Bastide de Capelongue* has seventeen Provençally decorated rooms, each of which bears the name of a well-known person from the Provence, whereas *La Ferme de Capelongue*, an old farm building, has fourteen stately and minimalistic apartments and a large garden. And finally, *Le Galinier de Lourmarin* is a fortress from the seventeenth century with twelve rooms and a large oblong swimming pool in the middle of a garden with age-old cedar, olive and pine trees. On the estate you also find a large botanical garden with vegetables, fruit and aromatic spices, and a biological garden with olive trees.

Edouard Loubet himself is at the head of the star restaurant of the same name. During the four summer months, a second restaurant is also open, *Le 4Months*. There, in the shade of the cedar trees and near the large swimming pool, you can enjoy a *table d'été* with light, Provençal dishes.

WITH THE CHEF'S OWN TOUCH...

MUSSELS IN A WHITE WINE SAUCE WITH CORIANDER

INGREDIENTS

For 6 people

3 kg mussels
1 onion
2 shallots
10 coriander pods
3 juniper berries
salt and pepper

Sauce

cooking fluid from the mussels
2 dl dry white wine
2 dl milk
2 dl liquid cream
1 handful of coriander
salt

PREPARATION

Wash the mussels in plenty of water and scrape them clean with a knife.

Peel and chop the onion and the shallots. Sauté them gently in a large steel pot and add the drained mussels. Cook thoroughly.

Add the coriander pods and the juniper berries, douse with white wine and cover the pot with a lid until all the mussels have opened. Remove the mussels from their shells and keep the cooking fluid for the sauce.

For the sauce, bring the white wine to the boil and allow it to reduce by one-third. Add the cooking fluid from the mussels, the milk and the cream. Bring back to the boil for a few minutes and then pour over half the coriander leaves. The remaining half will be used for decoration.

Édouard Loubet was born in Val Thorens and grew up in two different worlds: the world of top-class skiing and the world of the family hotel business. He has worked in a number of prestige kitchens, including Alain Chapel and Marc Veyrat. In 2005 Édouard moved his restaurant from Le Moulin de Lourmarin to Bonnieux, where he opened the Domaine de Capelongue. For Édouard Loubet the choice of products is not only an essential starting-point but also the basis for his cooking philosophy: vegetables from his own garden, home-made bread, etc. 'Pure and simple' is his motto.

MORE
than just a hotel

EDOUARD LOUBET

The philosophy and soul that Edouard Loubet was able to give the Bastide de Capelongue shows that he is a man of passion and persistence. He shares his love for delicious food with everyone who likes gastronomy through his cooking lessons and his books. In addition he has planted a biological and plant garden in the village and takes his guests along on outings to pick herbs in the Luberon.

WORTH DISCOVERING

The wine estate 'Val Joanis'

This sublime AOC wine estate in the Luberon dates from Roman times and for centuries was in the possession of the Joanis family. In 1978 it was purchased by a certain Cécile Chancel, who planted splendid gardens on three levels. The whole is perfectly integrated in the vineyards and separated by little authentic Roman walls. *'Val Joanis'* is recognised as one of the twelve most beautiful gardens in France.

LA BASTIDE DE MARIE

This elegant fortress from the eighteenth century is located in the Luberon between Gordes and Menèrbes.
It is the property of Jocelyne and Jean-Louis Sibuèt, who also have the Villa Marie in Saint-Tropez among other places.
The couple wanted to create a fairy-tale decor in the Bastide de Marie, but at the same time to preserve the look of an authentic Provençal farmhouse. The result is stunning.
A beautiful cypress-lined drive running past lavender fields leads you to the Bastide. Inside everything emits a cosy homey atmosphere, from the carefully chosen antique furniture to the monumental open hearth. For romantic adventurers *La Roulette* is recommended. In the caravan you stay in real gypsy style, with of course all the luxury and comfort of a five-star hotel.
The fish ponds of the past have been transformed into two swimming pools, one of which has been integrated among the rocks of the Bastide, and another is located in the garden with a view of the vineyards.
You can enjoy the delicious cuisine on the romantic pavement under an old linden tree or in the beautiful restaurant inside the fortress. Be sure not to miss the aperitif hour, when in the pavement dining area you are served *Le Jabugo*, a ham from the region, and other specialities with a delicious wine from Domaine de Marie.

WITH THE CHEF'S OWN TOUCH...

GAMBA TOASTS WITH A CREAM OF CANDIED TOMATOES, LES BAUX OLIVES, CAPERS AND PURSLANE SHOOTS

INGREDIENTS

For 4 people

1 kg vine tomatoes

4 slices of Poilâne bread

20 large gambas

50 g pitted black olives

10 g capers

1 tablespoon Parmesan cheese

1 clump of purslane

1 dl olive oil

salt, pepper and sugar

PREPARATION

Prepare the candied tomatoes by cutting the tomatoes into quarters (8), and placing them in an oven dish. Add a pinch of salt, pepper and sugar and dress with a dash of olive oil. Cook in the oven for about 6 hours at 80 °C. Mix half of the tomatoes until they form a smooth cream.

Toast the bread and keep it to one side for later.

Cook the gambas in a pan for 2 minutes on a high heat.

Spread the tomato cream on the toasted bread and then place the gambas, capers, olives and Parmesan cheese on top. Bake for 5 minutes in an oven at 180 °C.

Cut each slice of toast into three.

Add the rest of the candied tomatoes and decorate with the purslane shoots.

The chef at La Bastide de Marie, Laurent Houdart, is someone who is very close to nature and loves to work with seasonal products. For him, freshness is of the greatest importance. He visits his local market every morning, always in search of the very best ingredients from local producers. The contents of their stalls provide him with the inspiration for his menu of the day. Simple recipes and creative combinations give his cooking a light and melodious touch, packed full of flavour. This is a side of Provence that you will really want to taste!

MORE
than just a hotel

DOMAINE DE MARIE

This wine estate originated from the passion of Jean-Louis Sibuèt, the owner of La Bastide de Marie. When the Sibuèts purchased the bastide and the wine estate, Jean-Louis retained only the best old vines of the grape types *grenache* and *syrah*. He had the poorest quality vines replaced by new types such as *roussane, vermantino, cinsault and mourvèdre*. Here two white wines, one rosé and three red wines are produced, all with the AOC quality mark of the Luberon.

WORTH DISCOVERING

The lavender museum

In Coustellet, at the foot of the hills of the Luberon, we find the Lavender Museum housing the largest collection copper distillery vats in the world. A film tells the story of the whole production process in the Château du Bois, a lavender estate near Apt that works closely with the museum and alone supplies 10 percent of the French lavender production. The museum teaches you everything about the harvest, the distillation, the botanical aspects and the history of lavender.

In the shop of the museum you will be amazed by the large number of products based on the lavender plant, including oil, soap, bath creams and countless other wellness and beauty products.

18

LA COQUILLADE

This luxury hotel with its six buildings formed at one time a hamlet on the top of the hill of La Coquillade.
The estate has produced wine since the thirteenth century and is known as a resting place for migrating birds on their journey south or north. One of them is the lark or *couquihado* in Provençal from which the hotel gets its name.
In 2007 a Swiss financier bought the little village of Andreas Rihs with the wine estate and transformed it into an exclusive Relais & Châteaux hotel that under the label *Aureto* produces delicious AOC Côte Ventoux wines.
The estate has been restored with respect for the authenticity of the site and the building is finished off using only high-quality materials.
In La Coquillade respect for ecology is central, which resulted in the hotel being given the European Ecolabel.
A hot spring is the main source of energy in addition to solar energy and gas.
The extremely luxurious rooms were designed by great names such as Starck, Manutti and Dedon, and Frey.
There are even three different restaurants where you can sample the local cuisine: restaurant *Gourmet* for a general gastronomic menu, *Bistrot* for traditional regional dishes, and *Jardin des Vignes* near the vineyards for a pure and summer cuisine.
On this estate, thanks to its exceptional location on one of the mountain ridges of the Vaucluse, you can enjoy magnificent views of Mont Ventoux and the Luberon.

WITH THE CHEF'S OWN TOUCH...
CREAM OF JERUSALEM ARTICHOKE WITH TRUFFLE AND MIKADOS

INGREDIENTS

For 4 people

2 Jerusalem artichokes
800 cl milk
truffle flakes
4 g agaragar
40 g flour (T65)
8 g baker's yeast
4 g semolina
a little salt
20 cl water
40 cl olive oil
a pinch of Parmesan powder

PREPARATION

Cream of Jerusalem artichoke

Peel the artichokes. Keep 40 g to one side for later and boil the remainder in the milk with some truffle flakes. When cooked, spoon off 20 cl of the milk and keep to one side for later. Mix the rest to a smooth consistency.

Artichoke crisps

Cut the raw artichoke into fine slices using a mandolin. Deep fry the slices in oil at 120 °C.

Mikados

Mix together all the remaining ingredients, except the salt, until they form a homogenous paste. When this has been obtained, add the salt. Allow to rest for 20 minutes. Divide into portions of 40 g and roll into thin rods (do not allow the mixture to rise a second time). Bake for 3 minutes in an oven at 150 °C, until crisp and dry.

Take 40 g of the artichoke cream and add the agaragar. Dip the mikados in the sticky cream until well covered and then grate some truffle flakes over them.

Pour the warm artichoke cream into a cup.
Boil the other portion of milk and allow it to froth, before pouring on top of the artichoke cream.
Cut some roundels of truffle and arrange them with the artichoke crisps.

The rich and creative cuisine of Christophe Renaud is packed with the varied flavours of the South, and he offers his guests the chance to wipe their plates clean with a slice of his delicious home-made bread. His hallmark is refined cooking with plenty of vegetables, authentic tastes and fresh regional products: olive oil and biologically-grown poultry from Lubéron, fish from the Mediterranean Sea... His aromatic herbs and flowers come from his own bio-garden on the Domaine de la Coquillade.

MORE
than just a hotel

....

CAVE AURETO

This estate of thirty hectares is the property of
La Coquillade and vinifies AOC wines of the Ventoux
and the Luberon. The vineyards are located on the
sun-rich south-eastern slope of the hotel property
with a soil of clay and limestone. An oenological path
runs from the hotel through the *Aureto* estate, which
means 'soft breeze' in Provençal. During the walk you
will learn more about nature, the grape types,
the Aureto wines and the vinification process.
The wines can be sampled in the super-modern and
high-technology wine cellar, and each Wednesday
you can go for a walk with an oenologist. On Fridays it
is possible to participate in an exclusive wine tasting
in the tasting atelier.

....

WORTH DISCOVERING
Bicycle paradise

Each year, the region around Mont Ventoux draws tens of thousands of cycle tourists. Cycling events shoot up like mushrooms. La Coquillade has made good use of this sportive trend. In the hotel you will find the *'Provence Cycling Paradise,'* a showroom of no less than two-hundred square metres, sponsored by the exclusive Swiss bicycle brand BMC. The shop sells BMC accessories for the bicycle tourist and rents out bicycles and mountain bikes with which you can explore the magnificent region and perhaps climb the 1912 metre high 'Giant of the Provence.'

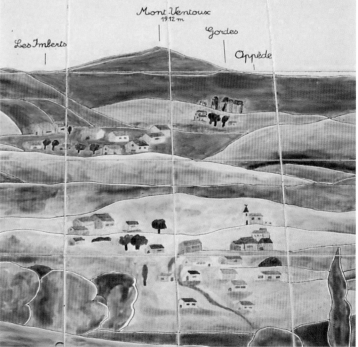

19

LA BASTIDE DE MOUSTIERS

'During a motorcycle trip through the Provence in 1994 I discovered an estate that was surrounded by lavender fields and olive groves. First I made it into my private home before I decided to share the Bastide with others. The estate still has a special place in my heart and that will always be so,' says Alain Ducasse.

The Bastide de Moustiers is located in the heart of the Alpes de Haute-Provence and previously was the residence of a *'maitre faïencier'* or a master faience manufacturer, *the* traditional speciality of Moustiers-Sainte-Marie. This nearby village is located at the end of the Gorges du Verdon, a hundred-seventy-five kilometre long gorge that separates the Var from the Alpes de Haute-Provence. Here the bright blue pure mountain water of the Verdon flows first into the gigantic Lac de Sainte-Croix before it empties into the Mediterranean Sea.
The Bastide is located in the midst of this magnificent natural beauty. The hotel-restaurant is surrounded by a park of four hectares where, along unpaved pathways, you can discover the old olive trees and art works of the estate.
Star chef Alain Ducasse entrusted the interior design of the Bastide to interior designer Tonia Peyrot who was able to give the whole an authentic aura. An example of her subtle taste is a discrete sign hanging on the door of the rooms that says: *'Laissez-nous écouter les cigales'* or *'Let us listen to the cicadas.'*

WITH THE CHEF'S OWN TOUCH...

HEARTH-ROASTED RIB OF BEEF WITH PLEASING PORTIONS OF SEASONAL VEGETABLES

INGREDIENTS

For 4 people
800 g rib of beef
8 carrots
1 celeriac
4 turnips with their tops
1 broccoli
a dash of olive oil
salt
roughly-ground pepper
80 g roasting juices

PREPARATION

Peel the carrots, celeriac and turnips.

Braise each vegetable separately in a pan with a little olive oil. If necessary, add a little vegetable stock towards the end of the cooking time.

Remove the broccoli roses and cook them in the English manner. Refresh in ice-cold water.

Clean the rib of beef and remove the fat.

Brush the meat with olive oil and sprinkle with salt.

Roast both sides of the meat over a charcoal fire, for as long as is necessary to achieve the desired cuisson.

Place the meat on a grille and allow it to rest for the same length of time it was cooked.

Season with rough-ground pepper before serving.

Serve the rib of beef whole on a serving platter, surrounded by the vegetables, or serve separate portions of meat and vegetables neatly arranged on individual plates.

La Bastide de Moustiers offers cooking for everyone. The pots give off the most delicious aromas, the meat is sizzling in the hearth, the kitchen staff are pleasantly busy and the chef is always happy to give a little added explanation about his menu of the day. The cuisine is Provencal and the suggestions board is changed daily. The rich and respectful cooking has just one objective: to make the very best use of the available seasonal products. Chef Christophe Martin finds his inspiration in the wide range of regional produce that the South has to offer. And with every dish he tells a different culinary story...

MORE
than just a hotel

....

LES JARDINS

Alain Ducasse put himself into his garden completely.
*'I wanted to lay out several gardens around the bastide
where everyone could do some exploring and where my
chefs could find an abundance of ingredients such as
herbs, vegetables and spices, which they could include in
their recipes.'*

The result was an aromatic herb garden, a garden for
salads, one with medicinal herbs, a garden with carrots and potatoes, and a *'wild garden,'* where you find
a mixture of spinach, cherry tomatoes, courgettes and
even sun flowers. Each day you will find the chefs
there and you can speak with them.

....

WORTH DISCOVERING

The faience museum

Moustiers-Sainte-Marie is known for its faience. In the seventeenth century, an Italian monk from Faenza taught a local potter how to make ceramics with a shiny layer of glaze. Since then Moustiers-Sainte-Marie has been the capital of faience.

The faience museum was established in 1929 by, among others, Marcel Provence, master faiencer of the Académie de Moustiers. In five halls, four-hundred antique and modern creations are on display. A film tells more about Moustiers as the faience centre of the world and about the production process through the centuries.

LE COUVENT DES MINIMES

Marquis Melchior de Forbin Janson built this monastery in 1613 for the order of *Les Minimes*. At that time the maintenance and cultivation of the herb garden occupied a large part of the day's activity.

After the French Revolution, the monastery remained vacant until Canon Terrasson restored it in 1862 and established an orphans home there. A few years later the Franciscan missionary sisters occupied the cloister and, in addition to their mission work, assumed responsibility for the maintenance and arrangement of the herbs garden. With the profit from it they financed their orphans' home and work.

The sisters left the cloister at the end of the twentieth century, which occasioned the beginning of the hotel *Le Couvent des Minimes & Spa*.

It is remarkable that the luxurious atmosphere of the five-star hotel on the one hand can go together so harmoniously with the devout and sober monastery style on the other hand.

Guests can choose between two restaurants. In *Le Cloître* a gastronomic cuisine is emphasised whereas the bistro *Le Pesquier* offers healthful, light regional dishes. In *La Cornue*, the wine cellar, wine and cheese tasting sessions are organised.

The herb garden is still cultivated and commercialised. On the estate you also find several hectares of botanical gardens with Mediterranean plants and herbs for the production of the cosmetics brand L'Occitane.

WITH THE CHEF'S OWN TOUCH...

FILLETED SARDINES WITH MARINATED PINEAPPLE TOMATOES AND A TANDOORI OF SWEET ONION AND PARMESAN.

INGREDIENTS

For 4 people

12 small sardines from the Mediterranean Sea

2 pineapple tomatoes

20 g grated Parmesan cheese

12 g sherry vinegar

25 g olive oil

80 g sweet onion

5 g tandoori spices

15 g raisins

10 g sherry vinegar

1 clove of garlic

salt and white pepper

NB:
Ask the fishmonger to leave the tails on the sardines.

PREPARATION

Sweet onion tandoori

Peel the onion, chop it finely and sauté in a large steel pan with a little olive oil on a low heat. Do not allow the onion to colour. Season lightly with salt and pepper and allow to braise slowly. When nearly cooked, stir in the tandoori spices, the raisins and the vinegar.
Taste and season accordingly.

Marinated sardines

Arrange the sardines on a plate. Season with salt and pepper, add the chopped garlic and sherry vinegar, and finish with a little olive oil. Keep in a cool place.

Pineapple tomatoes

Bring some water to the boil in a large cooking pot. Remove the stems from the tomatoes and immerse them for 15 seconds in the boiling water. Remove, clean and refresh in ice-cold water. Cut into round slices, 4 mm thick.

Presentation

Place two or three slices of tomato (depending on their thickness) on a flat plate. Cover with four spoonfuls of tandoori onion and place a marinated sardine on top of each portion of tomato. Pour over some of the marinade. Grate some Parmesan cheese over each sardine and sprinkle with tandoori herbs. Serve cool.

Since 11 June 2012 Jérôme Roy has taken charge of Le Cloître, a restaurant in a former Minim convent. His creed is 'let the products speak!' With just a little bit of creativity, Jérôme can evoke a wide range of culinary emotions.
He is a firm believer in a light and refined form of gastronomy, combined with plenty of flair, fabulous aromas and delicious flavours.
He does full justice to local products and is a strong advocate of authenticity. And his talents are not confined to the kitchen: the vegetable garden of the convent also contains dozens of different herbs, which he uses to give a traditional taste to his dishes.

MORE
than just a hotel

....

L' OCCITANE

The spa in the Couvent des Minimes uses the beauty products and perfumes of L'Occitane. This brand from the Alpes de Haute-Provence is made on the basis of local natural products such as lavender, honey, lemon plant and oils. During the last few years the brand has developed a complete range of spas in places such as Le Couvent des Minimes and in Paris.

....

WORTH DISCOVERING

L' Occitane & Le Prieuré de Salagon

This historically classified cloister has a garden of six hectares where about 2500 types of plants are grown. For centuries the Benedictine cloister sisters obtained medicinal extracts from the plants. The care and wellness brand L' Occitane used in the spa of Le Couvent des Minimes, sponsors the cloister and ethno botanical research to study the relation between humans and plants.

FIVE HOTEL & SPA

At the foot of the historic Notre-Dame-de-Bon-Voyage, where Napoleon lodged at one time, and right across from the fashionable Palais des Festival on the Croisette, now stands the luxurious design hotel Five Hotel & Spa. Studio Hertich & Adnet was responsible for the interior design and developed a concept that winks at the name of the church. One can see a collection of porcelain from all parts of the world. Drawings of imaginary landscapes and the painting *Carnets de Voyage Imaginaires* by Fabienne Jouvin cause you to dream of making a world tour.

The travel theme is continued in the spa where the five-star hotel works with the famous *Cinq Mondes* products, developed by world traveller Jean-Louis Poiroux who brings together in the label the best beauty rituals and products from all parts of the world.

The Sea Sens restaurant is located on the top floor and provides a magnificent view of the old part of the city, *Le Suquèt*. On the roof you can have a dip in the breath-taking overflow swimming pool with only the azure-blue sky as background.

WITH THE CHEF'S OWN TOUCH...

LINE-CAUGHT SEA BASS, FRIED ON ONE SIDE WITH WHITE MISO AND ACCOMPANIED BY VENUS CLAMS, A PUREE OF CARAMELISED CAULIFLOWER AND A YUZU MARMALADE

INGREDIENTS

For 4 people

600 g line-caught sea bass in filets

1 cauliflower

25 g yuzu marmalade

16 Venus clams

2 dl white wine

50 g shallot

20 g white miso paste

a dash of olive oil

2 dl cream

20 g butter

salt and freshly-ground white pepper

PREPARATION

Rinse the Venus clams thoroughly in water. Allow to drain.

Sauté the shallot and add the Venus clams and the white wine. Cover the pot and cook further.

Put the cooked Venus clams to one side for later.

Reduce the clams' cooking fluid and add 1 dl of cream. Season according to preference and mix well, until a smooth cream results.

Cook the cauliflower in the English manner (in salted water), and then allow it to colour briefly in a pan.

Keep the heart separate for the finishing.

Add 1 dl of cream, season according to preference and mix in a Thermomix. Glaze with a little butter.

Cut the sea bass into pieces of 150 g and score the skin side. Season according to preference.

Spread the miso paste over the meat side of the fish and then fry it on the skin side in olive oil.

Place a quenelle of the cauliflower puree on the plate and spread it open with a small spatula. Decorate with blobs of yuzu marmalade. Arrange the sea bass, Venus clams and some thin slices of raw cauliflower neatly on the plate. Finish with a piece of caramelised cauliflower and the Venus clam cream.

In the Sea Sens Restaurant of the Five Hotel & Spa, chef Arnaud Tabarec is able to display all his many culinary skills. The gastronomic 'market cuisine' that he offers is of outstanding quality.

His menu card amazes and surprises, as he takes his guests on a voyage of food discovery, artfully flavoured with herbs, spices and plants that often come from Asia. The perfectly balanced tastes seem familiar, but somehow they are always just that little bit different....

MORE
than just a hotel

INTUITIONS BY J

As world pastry champion, Chef Jérôme has developed a unique concept with '*Intuitions by J*,' a broad assortment of desserts. His workplace is housed in the Five Hotel & Spa, but it has a display window that opens to the street so you can buy or taste the desserts as in a regular shop. It is a real paradise for people with a sweet tooth.

WORTH DISCOVERING
Le Coca IV

Five Hotel & Spa has a twenty-seven metre long Leopard yacht in the harbour of Cannes that is exclusively for the use of its guests. Depending on the wishes of the customer, the yacht can be used for water-skiing in the bay or to sail to Saint-Tropez, and a romantic dinner on the water among the *'Iles de Lérins'* off the coast of Cannes is highly recommended. According to legend, the 'man with the iron mask,' the twin brother of Louis XIV, was imprisoned on Ile Sainte-Marguérite, the largest of the two islands. On the other island, Saint-Honorat, one of the most important monasteries of the Christian world is found, where monks still make wine and liquor.

22

CAP D'ANTIBES BEACH HOTEL

This beach hotel is a bit of paradise on earth where you can walk directly from your bedroom across the sandy beach and take a dip in the azure blue Mediterranean Sea. Cap d'Antibes Beach Hotel, on the Cap d'Antibes peninsula, is located near the fishermen's harbour, *Port des Pêcheurs*, and is not immediately noticeable with its modern, discrete low construction. As soon as you walk in, however, you find yourself in a sea of light and space, with fresh colours and beautiful design furniture.

The twenty-seven rooms and suites are individualised with trendy maritime wall drawings. Each room has a private pavement or garden and a view of the sea with the ochre-coloured Estérel mountain range as background.

In between, there is only the large swimming pool, the restaurants and the private beach.

The restaurant *Les Pêcheurs* serves daily-fresh *fruits de mer* and fish from the Mediterranean Sea, and during the summer months in *Le Cap* you can have lunch or dinner with your feet in the sand. Exceptional are the discrete orange tents on the beach that house *Summer Beach Wellness* with *La Colline* products.

Fine cooking over many years has ensured that Les Pêcheurs has an excellent reputation. This is largely the work of Philippe Jégo, who has been recognised by the Michelin Guide as a star-chef and in 2000 was chosen as the Meilleur Ouvrier de France. Philippe loves the flavours of the South. He does everything he possibly can to treat his guests to a sun-filled menu.

WITH THE CHEF'S OWN TOUCH...

GILLARDEAU OYSTERS WITH THE FLAVOURS OF THE SOUTH: ARTICHOKE, CÉBETTES, BOLETUS MUSHROOMS, PARMESAN CHEESE, CAVIAR, LEMON FROM MENTON, HAZELNUTS AND BASIL

INGREDIENTS

For 4 people

12 Gillardeau n° 3 oysters

Oysters with boletus mush-rooms

8 small boletus mushrooms ('Bouchon')

2 grey shallots

2 cloves of garlic

10 cl white Provence wine

1 lemon from Menton

1 red mini-paprika

Espelette pepper

1 bouquet garni

a few coriander pods

fennel seeds and white peppercorns

capers with stem

extra virgin olive oil

Oysters with artichoke

4 purple artichokes

1 orange

1 white onion

10 cl poultry stock

1 cl white balsamic vinegar

fresh basil

extra virgin olive oil

Parmesan cheese, well-aged 'Parmiggiano Reggiano'

cherry tomatoes

edible flowers from the rose geranium

Oysters with caviar from Aquitaine

1 young leek (white part only)

2 cébettes

1 small fennel

burnt hazelnut oil

20 g 'Rare de Perlita' caviar

Szechuan pepper

borage flowers

PREPARATION

Open the oysters, remove them from the shells and keep them in their own juices in a cool place. Clean the shells, dry them and put them on a plate.

Oysters with boletus mushrooms

Sauté the finely diced shallot and onion in olive oil, then add the chopped mushrooms. Pour in the lemon juice and the white wine. Add the bouquet garni. Season and allow to cook for 10 minutes. Blanch the lemon peel three times and then boil in salted water with the mini-paprika. Allow to cool. Fill the shells with the boletus mixture and place an oyster, with a little juice, on top of each one. Finish with a tasteful garnish of lemon and paprika.

Oysters with artichoke

Cut the heads off the artichokes, boil them in the poultry stock and then cut the leaves into fine strips. Sauté a diced onion in olive oil. Add the orange juice, balsamic vinegar and a few basil leaves. Marinate the artichoke strips in this mixture. Allow to cool. Fill each shell with the artichoke strips, add an oyster, some juice and some of the reduced marinade to each one. Finish with some flakes of Parmesan cheese, pieces of cherry tomato, some basil leaves and rose geranium flowers.

Oysters with 'Rare de Perlita' caviar from Aquitaine

Stew the leek white, *cébettes* and borage flowers in hazelnut oil. Add some of the oyster juice and allow to reduce. When cool, fill the shells with this mixture, add an oyster and some juice to each one, and finish with a small spoonful of caviar, the crispy fennel heart and the borage flowers.

MORE
than just a hotel

....

RESTAURANT LES PÊCHEURS

This gastronomic restaurant is known for its delicious spicy, grilled fish dishes. This culinary pearl lies hidden in the small fishermen's harbour and, because of its unique location, it treats its guests to delectable tastes and an unforgettable evening.

....

WORTH DISCOVERING

Cap d'Antibes

The coast of the peninsula is strewn with white, eroded rocks.
The so-called *'Sentier des Douaniers'* runs along here, a well-known walking path that customs officials used in the past to patrol for smugglers. Today you only hear the cry of the seagulls and the sound of the sea. On one side you have a view of the impressive villas and gardens, on the other side you look out over the bay and the coast of the Côte d'Azur. Here Jules Verne found inspiration for his *'Twenty Thousand Leagues Under The Sea.'*
This exceptional peninsula has an exceptional history behind it. Since the first half of the twentieth century it has been an attraction for great names such as Greta Garbo, King Leopold of Belgium, and Onassis.

LA BASTIDE SAINT-ANTOINE

The perfume capital, Grasse, is nestled on the slopes of the Alpes Maritimes and is located, as the crow flies, about fifteen kilometres from the Mediterranean Sea near the Italian border. Right below this historic city, removed from all pressures, La Bastide Saint Antoine enjoys a magnificent view of the bay of Cannes and the Estérel mountains. The patron is the star chef, Jacques Chibois, who first gained experience with top chefs such as Roger Vergé and Michel Guérard before he opened his own luxury hotel and restaurant in 1996. Great stars, from the Kennedys to the Rolling Stones, have lodged here. The rooms bear the names of the picturesque villages in the Provençal hinterland between the Côte d'Azur and Grasse, such as Opio, Peymeinade and Saint-Vallier, which illustrates the personal approach of the hotel. The illustrious chef with his refined cuisine is, however, the greatest drawing card of this Relais & Châteaux. In the pavement dining area, during the summer months, you can enjoy his culinary creations in a splendid garden full of olive trees and elegant garden sculptures.

RELAIS &
CHATEAUX

Jacques Chibois
GRAND CHEF

WITH THE CHEF'S OWN TOUCH...
COFFEE FOAM WITH GOLD LEAF AND ALMOND FLOWERS

INGREDIENTS

For 4 people

360 g double cream

20 g coffee beans

80 g meringue (3 egg whites, 90 g sugar and a dash of lemon juice)

Finishing

Some pinches of ground coffee

4 pieces of gold leaf

some almond flowers

(or rose petals or some other white flower)

Sauce

160 g double cream

10 g Amaretto

20 g sugar

a few drops of lemon juice

PREPARATION

Meringue

Pre-heat the oven to 110 °C. Boil some water in a large steel pan. Place a large dish containing the egg white, sugar and lemon juice into the boiling water. Beat with a mixer until the meringue has achieved the perfect consistency (it should form a point on the end of the whisk). Pipe out bars of the meringue mixture onto grease-free paper, using a piping bag with a nozzle diameter of 5 mm to 8 mm. Place in the oven for 2 to 3 hours, until crisp and dry. Cut the meringues into 1 cm pieces. Cooks using a hot-air oven should weigh down the grease-free paper, so that it cannot move.

Foam

Crush the coffee beans roughly with a rolling pin or the bottom of a steel pan. Allow the groundings to soak for 5 minutes in 160 g of double cream that has been heated for no longer than 1 minute. Allow to cool.
Mix with the rest of the cream, which has first been beaten to a smooth and thick consistency.
Add the pieces of meringue. Serve this dessert 10 minutes after preparation.

Sauce

Place the cream, Amaretto and lemon juice in a bowl, beat with a whisk and carefully add the sugar.

Presentation

Divide into four portions, with a piece of gold leaf in the middle of each one. Brush some sauce onto the surface of the plates. Decorate with flowers and ground coffee.

This maestro is a true professional: a rough diamond with a heart of pure gold. This expert in olive oil (he makes his own) and truffle (which he employs in all its different forms) makes use of all the richness that both the land and the sea can offer. The fresh fruit from local gardens gives a distinctive edge to his cooking. His gastronomic menus are a deliciously light symphony of flavours and textures. His dishes exude the aromas and tastes of high-quality products prepared with respect and great refinement.

MORE
than just a hotel

WITH JACQUES CHIBOIS IN THE KITCHEN

In the Bastide de Saint-Antoine you can take cooking lessons from Jacques Chibois and his team. You may even help them and then eat your own self-prepared meal at the *table d'hôte*. It is a special experience for anyone who would like to find out what goes on behind the scenes in a star restaurant.

WORTH DISCOVERING
Parfumerie Fragonard

In the heart of Grasse you find *'Parfumerie Fragonard,'* possibly the best known perfumery in the world, which has its own museum. The authentic factory is one of the oldest in Grasse. The owners decided in 1926 to rename the factory 'Fragonard,' after the famous painter Jean-Honoré Fragonard.

In the museum you learn how perfume is made, and during a special introductory lesson you can formulate your own perfume. Afterwards, those who took the course are invited to a special lunch emphasising perfume aromas with Jacques Chibois in the Bastide Saint-Antoine.

LE MAS CANDILLE

This Relais & Châteaux, surrounded by stately cypress and olive trees and with a panoramic view of Grasse and the Pré-Alpes du Sud, is a little paradise on earth. Le Mas Candille gets its name from the Provençal word for candle-holder, *candille*, because the soldiers during the French Revolution used the cypresses as an orientation point.
The hotel complex consists of three buildings: the *Villa Candille* with six contemporarily decorated suites, the *Bastide* with nineteen elegant rooms, and the eighteenth-century *farmhouse*, with twenty romantic *chambres de charme*.
In this last building, olives and wine were processed in the past.
The interior of the gastronomic restaurant *Le Candille*, with its classic furniture, takes the rich past of the farmhouse into consideration. The showpiece is the ceiling painting that depicts the sky in all of its colours and shapes, and pays tribute to a well-known person from the region, Jean Honoré Fragonard, an eighteenth-century painter who introduced the romantic period. In the second restaurant, *La Pergola*, next to the swimming pool, you can have breakfast or enjoy a light lunch. If you stand in the pavement dining area of Le Mas Candille at sunset and see the last sunlight give a honey yellow hue to the Mediterranean peripheral wall and the cypresses, you can easily imagine that you are in *La Bella Italia*.

WITH THE CHEF'S OWN TOUCH...

EGG SURPRISE, WITH SHREDS OF BLUE LOBSTER AND AN IODISED FOAM

INGREDIENTS

1 per person

Egg surprise
5 egg yolks
12 egg whites
1 teaspoon white vinegar

Lobster
A soup of different vegetables
(carrot, fennel, leek, paprika,
star aniseed, coriander,
coarse salt)
Canadian lobster (½ lobster of
600 g, or 3 pieces for 5 people)

Lobster soup foam
(3 dl per person)
lobster shell (carcass)
½ carrot, finely diced
½ leek, finely diced
1 teaspoon tomato puree
1 onion, finely diced
½ fennel, finely diced

PREPARATION

Surprise egg

Separate the eggs. Grease a semi-circular Flexipan (sufficiently large) with butter.
Beat the fresh and dry egg white with a pinch of salt. Finish with the vinegar and use immediately. Completely grease the inside of the round baking dish and spread out the egg yolks in the bottom. Cover with the rest of the egg white and place in an oven for 6 minutes at 95 °C. Remove immediately from the baking dish and place in a new dish. Cover with a sheet of greased baking paper and warm for 3 minutes in a steam oven.

Lobster

Make a flavoursome soup with the different vegetables. Place the lobster in the pot, so that the tail is in an upright position.
Boil for 4 minutes in the soup and then refresh in ice-cold water, so that the cooking process is halted. Remove the claws and cook them for a further 2 minutes in the soup. Keep the shells of the carcass separately to make the lobster soup. Remove the meat from the claws, ensuring that there are no tough pieces of cartilage.
Also keep the innermost parts of the shells to make the lobster soup, as well as the heads and legs (for decoration).

Lobster soup foam

Crush the lobster shells as finely as possible and colour them in warm olive oil. Add the aromatic garniture (pre-mixed in a kitchen robot) and the tomato puree. Cover with water and bring to the boil. Mix, pass through a conical sieve and keep the liquid to one side for later. Adjust the seasoning as required and work up into a foam at the moment of serving.

Presentation

As in the photograph. Decorate with the lobster heads and legs, and some shiso.

Serge Gouloumès became chef at Le Mas Candille in April 2001. Four years later, he was able to add a first star to his already impressive record of achievements. He prepares typically southern cuisine (Italian and Provencal) with interesting herbal accents and more than a passing nod to the region of his birth: Gascogne.

MORE
than just a hotel

SPA SHISEIDO

The Shiseido treatments date from in the nineteenth century and are a symbiosis of eastern philosophy and western technology. The first spa opened in 2002 in Le Mas Candille. The massages are based on the Qi, the energy that makes the connection between body and mind. Each treatment begins with the selection of your own favourite aroma. You breath it in so you are relaxed and your spirit is made free. Architect Brigitte Dumont de Chassart designed the spa of Le Mas Candille completely according to the philosophy of Shiseido with a Japanese garden and restful water gardens. The interior design of the five treatment rooms is sober and Zen, and all rooms look out on the garden.

WORTH DISCOVERING

The photography museum

André Villers is one of the best-known photographers in the world *and* was a fellow villager of Picasso, whose distinctive head is often seen in the photos of Villers, in addition to other famous persons such as Miró, Dali, Léger, Le Corbusier and Chagall. Picasso often worked with Villers artistically. For example, he made photos that Picasso cut in pieces to make collages. One day the two artists decided to establish their own photo museum in 'their' Mougins. Not only can one see life on the Côte d'Azur in pictures, the museum also has a display of antique cameras and accessories.

25

LE SAINT-PAUL

You find the entrance to this Relais & Châteaux among the many art galleries in the picturesque Rue Grande of the mystical artist village, Saint-Paul-de-Vence. The first stone of this sixteenth-century building dates from 1511. Before private individuals lived in this stately mansion, it served as a hospital, church and meeting place for secret organisations that conspired against the regime of that time. Le Saint Paul officially opened its doors, after thorough renovation works in 1989, as the only hotel inside the walls of the city.

The Provençally decorated rooms look out over the Mediaeval roofs of the village and the magnificent landscape of the Côte d'Azur. The restaurant is housed in two cosy and snug rooms, the first decorated with beautiful fresco's and the second with an elegant fountain, which makes the choice difficult when you reserve. The decision is even more difficult when the weather is nice, because then you can lunch or dine in the pavement area next to the city wall with a view of the magnificent environment.

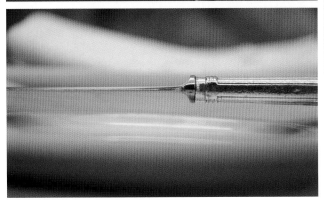

WITH THE CHEF'S OWN TOUCH...

CRÈME BRULÉE WITH WHITE CHOCOLATE, LEMON, CAPERS AND PISTACHIO NUTS

INGREDIENTS

For 4 people

Crème brulée with white chocolate

500 g liquid cream (35%)

3.5 g pectin (X58), 60 g sugar

75 g egg yolk, 100 g white chocolate 'Opalys', salted and candied lemon in blocks*

Pistachio madeleine

50 g butter, 62 g sugar

8 g brown sugar

38 g pistachio paste

8 g honey, 28 g egg yolk

55 g egg white, 75 g flour

2.5 g baking powder

0.5 g salt

Glazed sugar rolls with capers

125 g glazing sugar

75 g glucose, muesli powder*

dried caper powder*

Puree of candied lemon

60 g yellow lemon peel

100 g lemon juice, 50 g sugar

crushed pistachio nuts (decoration)

oregano leaves*

unsalted capers*

*quantity as preferred

PREPARATION

Crème brulée with white chocolate

Prepare the ingredients in the same manner as for a crème anglaise. Pour the cream through a conical sieve over the white chocolate. Mix thoroughly, but ensure that no air is beaten into the mixture. Add the blocks of candied lemon according to preference. Pour into semi-circular rings and harden in the freezer.

Pistachio madeleine

Blanch the butter, sugar and brown sugar. Add the pistachio paste and stir carefully. Next add the honey. Gently fold in the egg yolk and the egg white. Finally add the dry ingredients. Pour the mixture onto a 6 mm deep baking tray. Bake in the oven for 12 minutes at 190 °C. Allow to cool, then cut into oblongs measuring 9 cm by 3 cm.

Glazed sugar rolls with capers

Bake the glazing sugar and the glucose at 155 °C. Mix the two powders together. Pour onto a silicone pad and allow to cool. Grind the sugar into a fine powder, sprinkle it over the oblong madeleines and bake in the oven at 160 °C until they form crispy rolls.

Puree of sweet candied lemon

Blanch the lemon peel. Boil the peel with the juice and the sugar. Mix.

Laurent Paccini was born in Aix-en-Provence in 1976, the son of a traditional arts and crafts family, with a Provencal heart and Italian roots. He took his first tentative steps in gastronomy in Aix-en-Provence, Paris, Monte Carlo and Gardona Riviera in Italy. A lover of travel, his journeys to other places and his meetings with different cultures and unfamiliar peoples have stimulated his curiosity and his culinary thinking. 'In all simplicity, I wish to pay tribute in my cooking to my many teachers, from the most famous to the most humble.'

MORE
than just a hotel

....

LE SAINT-PAUL, WITH ART AS ITS THEME

No other hotel is so entwined with its Mediaeval city environment as Hotel Saint-Paul. Saint-Paul was discovered in 1920 by Signac, Modigliani, Matisse, Picasso and Chagall. Up to the present time, this artistic past continues to live, both in the hotel and in the city with its many art galleries. Thus it is an ideal destination for art enthusiasts, who among other things, can visit the grave of Chagall in the cemetery.

....

WORTH DISCOVERING

Fondation Maeght

Aimé Maeght was a great lover of art and a fervent admirer of Miró. At the beginning of the sixties he established a museum within walking distance from the city centre of Saint-Paul. The building, designed by Catalan architect, Joseph Lluis Sert, is a work of art itself.

In addition to works by artists such as Pol Bury, Braque and Miró, you also find an extremely valuable collection of paintings from the twentieth century, including works by Tapiès, Léger and Matisse.

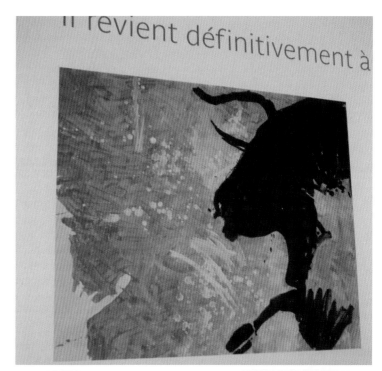

GRAND HÔTEL DU CAP FERRAT

The region around the Alpes-Maritimes is really breath-taking. Since 1908 this high-class, stately hotel has occupied the entire end of Cap-Ferrat, one of the greenest and most fascinating places of the region.

Even in its early years, the hotel attracted many famous people, such as Gustave Eiffel, Charlie Chaplin and Picasso. Each of them, after their visit, retained an unforgettable memory of the endless horizon, the salty sea breeze and the discrete and elegant luxury of the hotel.

Up to the present time, this five-star hotel that was restored in 2011, has remained an established value for many pleasure-lovers. It was not accidental that it was given the prestigious *Palace* award, issued by the French Ministry of Tourism.

Old and new elements form a nice balance: the nineteenth-century rotunda by Gustave Eiffel goes together perfectly with *La Résidence*, the new wing which houses a sublime spa. The swimming pool with Olympic airs dates from 1939 and can be reached with a private lift. Here, the daughter of Charlie Chaplin received her first swimming lesson from Pierre Grunberg, who is still active in the hotel.

Every one of the meals of *La Véranda* with its Mediterranean cuisine and of *Le Cap* with its gastronomic star cuisine is a feast for the senses. In *Le Salon des Collections* you find the largest and most expensive wine collection in the world including 141 bottles of Château d'Yquem and 33 bottles of Château Lafite Rothschild from 1799.

WITH THE CHEF'S OWN TOUCH...
VARIATIONS ON RAW AND COOKED VEGETABLES FROM THE MARKET

INGREDIENTS

For 4 people

1 purple carrot
1 yellow carrot
1 orange carrot with top
1 cauliflower
4 spring onions
1 celeriac
1 Hamburg parsley
4 purple artichokes
1 parsnip
1 stick of celery
rocket salad
(quantity as preferred)
spinach shoots
50 g Piccadilly tomatoes
1 bundle of green asparagus
1 bundle of red radishes
50 g fennel
bread crisps (4 fine slices,
cut with a meat-slicer)
50 g Taggia olives
130 g courgette

PREPARATION

Peel and slice the vegetables.
There is no hard-and-fast rule for the quantities
of vegetables or their methods of preparation. This is a
matter for the chef's own personal preference.
This is what our chef, Didier Aniès, recommends:
Cook the carrots, cauliflower and celery in the English
manner (in warm water with 10 g of coarse salt per litre).
Roast the spring onion, celeriac, Hamburg parsley,
artichoke, courgette and parsnip in olive oil.
Serve the remaining raw vegetables as a salad with a courgette cream, made from 15 g cooked and mixed courgette,
15 g white balsamic cream and 10 g olive oil.
The vegetables to be served raw are the green asparagus,
red radish, fennel, tomatoes and spinach shoots.
As an alternative to raw serving, the green asparagus
can be boiled in water.

Didier Aniès was born into a family of winegrowers in Limoux. In 1998 he was awarded his first star for his work in Restaurant Le Cagnard in Cagnes-sur-Mer. In 2000 he was chosen as Meilleur Ouvrier de France. He developed his talents to the full at Hotel Mirabeau in Monaco and in 2007 he took another major step forward in his career with his move to Grand Hôtel Cap-Ferrat, where just a year later he was also awarded a star. Didier's cuisine is classic. 'A chicken is a chicken,' he says. He is not an advocate of fusion cooking or molecular cooking. 'The purpose of my cooking is to surprise my guests by unexpected and daring combinations of flavours and products. But I don't discover anything new. I just cook.'

MORE
than just a hotel

LE SPA

This splinter-new spa, designed by Pierre-Yves Rochon, looks out on an immense garden and uses products of the exclusive *Bellefontaine* and *Carita*. The beautiful building is even more beautiful thanks to the impressive garden. When the weather is nice you can have your spa treatment in one of the five beautiful small pavilions.

WORTH DISCOVERING

Villa Ephrussi de Rothschild

At the beginning of the twentieth century, on the smallest part of the Cap Ferrat peninsula, Baroness Ephrussi de Rothschild had a stately villa built in Florentine-Moresque style. The view is breath-taking. Along the west side you look out over the bay of Villefranche, along the east side over the bay of Beaulieu. In the villa itself you find a large collection of art works. The baroness laid out seven gardens behind the palace, each with its own theme, going from an Italian, a Spanish and a Japanese garden to a rock garden, a Provençal, a French and a rose garden. In 1934 she gave the estate to the *'Institut de France'* and the villa became a museum.

AVIGNON

1. LA MIRANDE
4, Place Amirande
F.84000 Avignon
Tel (0033) (0) 490 14 20 20
mirande@la-mirande.fr
www.la-mirande.fr

2. LE PRIEURÉ
7, Pl Chapitre
F. 30400 Villeneuve-lès-Avignon
Tel (0033) (0) 490 15 90 15
contact@leprieure.com
www.leprieure.com

LES ALPILLES

3. MAISON BRU
Route d' Orgon
F. 13810 Eygalières
Tel (0033) (0) 490 60 34
reservations@chezbru.com
www.chezbru.com

4. OUSTAU DE BAUMANIÈRE
F. 13520 Les-Baux-de-Provence
Tel. (0033) (0) 490 54 33 07
contact@oustaudebaumaniere.com
www.oustaudebaumaniere.com

5. LA CABRO D' OR
F. 13520 Les-Baux-de-Provence
Tel. (0033) (0) 490 54 33 21
contact@lacabrodor.com
www.lacabrodor.com

LA CAMARGUE

6. LODGE DE LA FOUQUE
Route du Petit Rhône
F. 13460 Saintes-Maries-de-la-Mer
Tel. (0033) (0) 490 97 81 02
info@masdelafouque.com
www.masdelafouque.com

7. LE MAS DE PEINT
Le Sambuc
F. 13200 Arles
Tel. (0033) (0) 490 97 20 62
contact@masdepeint.com
www.lemasdepeint.com

AIX-EN-PROVENCE

8. VILLA GALLICI
18, Avenue de la Violette
F. 13100 Aix-en-Provence
Tel. (0033) (0) 442 23 29 23
reservation@villagallici.com
www.villagallici.com

VAR - SAINT-TROPEZ

9. HOSTELLERIE DE L' ABBAYE DE LA CELLE
10, Place du Général de Gaulle
F. 83170 La-Celle-en-Provence
Tel. (0033) (0) 498 05 14 14
contact@abbaye-celle.com
www.abbaye-celle.com

10. CHÂTEAU DE BERNE
Route de Lorgues
F. 83510 Lorgues
Tel. (0033) (0) 494 60 43 60
hotel@chateauberne.com
www.chateauberne.com

11. VILLA MARIE
Route des Plages
Chemin Val de Rian
F. 83350 Saint-Tropez
Tel. (0033) (0) 457 74 74 74
contact@villamarie.fr
www.villamarie.com

12. LA RÉSERVE DE RAMATUELLE
Chemin de la Quesinne
F. 83350 Ramatuelle
Tel. (0033) (0) 494 44 94 44
inforamatuelle@lareserve.ch
www.lareserve-ramatuelle.com

13. PAN DEÏ PALAIS
52, Rue Gambetta
F. 83990 Saint-Tropez
Tel. (0033) (0) 494 17 71 71
Saint-tropez@pandei.com
www.pandei.com

14. SEZZ
151, Route des Salins
F. 83990 Saint-Tropez
Tel. (0033) (0) 494 55 31 55
sainttropez@hotelsezz.com
www.hotelsezz.com

15. MUSE
Route des Marres
F. 83350 Ramatuelle
Tel. (0033) (0) 494 430 440
info@muse-hotels.com
www.muse-hotels.com

LE LUBÉRON

16. LA BASTIDE DE CAPELONGUE
Chemin des Cabanes
F. 84480 Bonnieux
Tel. (0033) (0) 490 75 89 78
reservation@capelongue.com
www.capelongue.com

17. LA BASTIDE DE MARIE
Route de Bonnieux
F. 84560 Ménerbes
Tel. (0033) (0) 457 74 74 74
contact@labastidedemarie.com
www.labastidedemarie.com

18. LA COQUILLADE
Le Perrotet
F. 84400 Gargas
Tel. (0033) (0) 490 74 71 71
info@coquillade.fr
www.coquillade.fr

ALPES DE HAUTE-PROVENCE

19. LA BASTIDE DE MOUSTIERS
Chemin des Quison
F. 04360 Moustiers-Sainte-Marie
Tel. (0033) (0) 492 70 47 47
contact@bastide-moustiers.com
www.bastide-moustiers.com

20. LE COUVENT DES MINIMES
Chemin des Jeux de Mai
F. 04300 Mane-en-Provence
Tel. (0033) (0) 492 74 77 77
reservations@couventdesminimes-hotelspa.com
www.couventdesminimes-hotelspa.com

ALPES MARITIMES

21. FIVE HOTEL & SPA
1, Rue Notre Dame
F. 06400 Cannes
Tel. (0033) (0) 463 36 05 05
info@five-hotel.com
www.five-hotel-cannes.com

22. CAP D' ANTIBES BEACH HOTEL
10, Boulevard Maréchal Juin
F. 06160 Antibes
Tel. (0033) (0) 492 93 13 13
contact@ca-beachhotel.com
www.ca-beachhotel.com

23. LA BASTIDE SAINT ANTOINE
48, Avenue Henri Dunant
F. 06130 Grasse
Tel. (0033) (0) 493 70 94 94
info@jacques-chibois.com
www.jacques-chibois.com

24. LE MAS CANDILLE
Boulevard Clément Rebuffel
F. 06250 Mougins
Tel. (0033) (0) 492 28 43 43
reservations@lemascandille.com
www.lemascandille.com

25. LE SAINT-PAUL
86, Rue Grande
F. 06570 Saint-Paul-de-Vence
Tel. (0033) (0) 493 32 65 25
reservation@lesaintpaul.com
www.lesaintpaul.com

26. GRAND HÔTEL DU CAP FERRAT
71, Boulevard du Général de Gaulle
F. 06230 Saint-Jean-Cap-Ferrat
Tel. (0033) (0) 493 76 50 50
reservation@ghcf.fr
www.grand-hotel-cap-ferrat.com

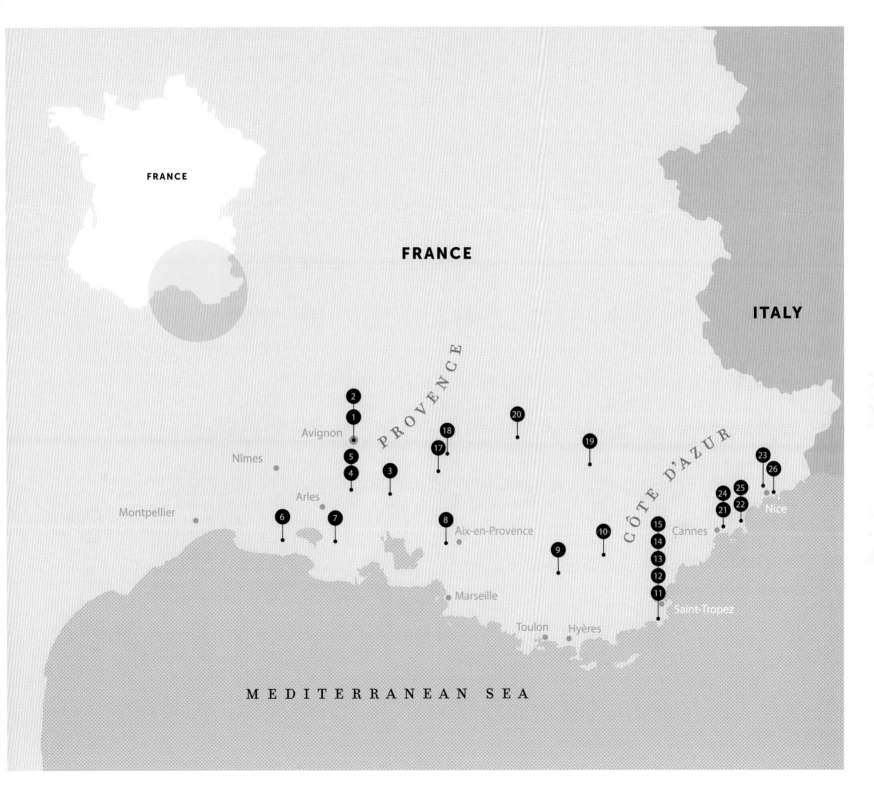

FRANCE

ITALY

PROVENCE

CÔTE D'AZUR

Avignon

Nîmes

Montpellier

Arles

Aix-en-Provence

Marseille

Toulon

Hyères

Cannes

Nice

Saint-Tropez

MEDITERRANEAN SEA

1
2
3
4
5
6
7
8
9
10
11
12
13
14
15
17
18
19
20
21
22
23
24
25
26

WEIGHTS FOR DRY INGREDIENTS

METRIC	IMPERIAL
7 g	¼ oz
15 g	½ oz
20 g	¾ oz
25 g	1 oz
40 g	1½ oz
50 g	2 oz
60 g	2½ oz
75 g	3 oz
100 g	3½ oz
125 g	4 oz
140 g	4½ oz
150 g	5 oz
165 g	5½ oz
175 g	6 oz
200 g	7 oz
225 g	8 oz
250 g	9 oz
275 g	10 oz
300 g	11 oz
350 g	12 oz
375 g	13 oz
400 g	14 oz
425 g	15 oz
450 g	1lb
500 g	1 lb 2 oz
550 g	1¼ lb
600 g	1 lb 5 oz
650 g	1 lb 7oz
675 g	1½ lb
700 g	1 lb 9 oz
750 g	1 lb 11 oz
800 g	1¾ lb
900 g	2 lb
1 kg	2¼ lb
1.1 kg	2½ lb
1.25 kg	2¾ lb
1.35 kg	3 lb
1.5 kg	3 lb 6 oz
1.8 kg	4 lb
2 kg	4½ lb
2.25 kg	5 lb
2.5 kg	5½ lb
2.75 kg	6 lb

LIQUID MEASURES

METRIC	IMPERIAL	US
25 ml	1 fl oz	
50 ml	2 fl oz	¼ cup
75 ml	3 fl oz	
100 ml	3½ fl oz	
120 ml	4 fl oz	½ cup
150 ml	5 fl oz	
175 ml	6 fl oz	¾ cup
200 ml	7 fl oz	
250 ml	8 fl oz	1 cup
300 ml	10 fl oz / ½ pint	1¼ cups
360 ml	12 fl oz	
400 ml	14 fl oz	
450 ml	15 fl oz	2 cups / 1 pint
600 ml	1 pint	2½ cups
750 ml	1¼ pints	
900 ml	1½ pints	
1 litre	1¾ pints	1 quart
1.2 litres	2 pints	
1.4 litres	2½ pints	
1.5 litres	2¾ pints	
1.7 litres	3 pints	
2 litres	3½ pints	
3 litres	5¼ pints	

OVEN TEMPERATURES

°C	°F
110	225
120	250
140	275
150	300
160	325
180	350
190	375
200	400
220	425
230	450
240	475

WWW.LANNOO.COM

Register on our web site and we will regularly send you a newsletter with information about new books and interesting, exclusive offers.

RECIPES: La Mirande (François Secrétin), Le Prieuré (Fabien Fage), Maison Bru (Wout Bru), Oustau de Baumanière (Sylvestre Wahid), La Cabro d'Or (Michel Hulin), Lodge de la Fouque (Frédérick Pelletier), Le Mas de Peint (Vincent Laisney), Villa Gallici (Christophe Gavot), Hostellerie de l'abbaye de la Celle (Benoit Witz), Château de Berne (Sébastien Nouveau), Villa Marie (Lionel Arnoux), La Réserve de Ramatuelle (Éric Canina), Pan deï Palais (Renaud Capelle), La Bastide de Capelongue (Édouard Loubet), La Bastide de Marie (Laurent Houdart), La Coquillade (Christophe Renaud), La Bastide de Moustiers (Christophe Martin), Le Couvent des Minimes (Jérôme Roy), Five Hotel & Spa (Arnaud Tabarec), Cap d'Antibes Beach Hotel (Philippe Jéga), La Bastide de Saint Antoine (Jacques Chibois), Le Mas Candille (Serge Gouloumès), Le Saint-Paul (Laurent Paccini) et le Grand-Hôtel du Cap-Ferrat (Didier Aniès)

TEXT: Luc Quisenaerts

ENGLISH TRANSLATION: Roy Davison and Ian Connerty

LAY-OUT: Inge Van Damme

CARTOGRAPHY: Wim Vandersleyen

If you have observations or questions, please contact our editorial office:
redactielifestyle@lannoo.com

©Uitgeverij Lannoo nv, Tielt, 2013

D/2013/45/221 – NUR 450

ISBN 978 94 014 0757 1

PHOTO CREDITS

COVER: Grégoire Gardette

INTRODUCTORY PHOTOS: Hendrik Biegs (except p4 Manuel Zublena)

LA MIRANDE: Hendrik Biegs, hôtel La Mirande

LE PRIEURÉ: Henk, G. Gardette, R. McKenna, J. Froc (p30 E.Morin – G.Gardette)

MAISON BRU: Hendrik Biegs (p39 Hervé Fabre)

L'OUSTAU DE BAUMANIÈRE: Hendrik Biegs, L. Parrault, G. Gardette, JP Gabriel, R. McKenna (p46 R.McKenna, V. Ovessian)

LA CABRO D'OR: JP. Gabriel, L. Parrault (p54-55 E. Beracassat, G. Gardette), Hendrik Biegs

LODGE DE LA FOUQUE: Clémence Fenninger, Hendrik Biegs

LE MAS DE PEINT: Bernard Touillon, Ange Lorente, Hervé Hotte, Henk Van Cauwenbergh

VILLA GALLICI: John Hesseltine

HOSTELLERIE DE L'ABBAYE DE LA CELLE: Hendrik Biegs

CHÂTEAU DE BERNE: Chris Wiedemann, Marion Gillet, Hendrik Biegs (p95)

VILLA MARIE: Hendrik Biegs

LA RÉSERVE DE RAMATUELLE: Grégoire Gardette, Hendrik Biegs (food)

PAN DEÏ PALAIS: Marcel Jolibois, Hendrik Biegs

SEZZ: Manuel Zublena, Aqua di Parma spa Anthony Lanneretonne°

MUSE: Véronique Mati

LA BASTIDE DE CAPELONGUE: JM Favre

LA BASTIDE DE MARIE: Hendrik Biegs

LA COQUILLADE: hotel La Coquillade

LA BASTIDE DE MOUSTIERS: Hendrik Biegs

LE COUVENT DES MINIMES: Hendrik Biegs – Tania Hillion

FIVE HOTEL & SPA: Marc el Jolibois, Anaël Joli, Aline Gérard

CAP D'ANTIBES BEACH HOTEL: Hendrik Biegs, hôtel Cap d'Antibes

LA BASTIDE SAINT-ANTOINE: Didier Bouko

LE MAS CANDILLE: Hendrik Biegs, picture chef and dish d'Anthony Carvalho.

LE SAINT-PAUL: Hendrik Biegs

GRAND-HÔTEL DU CAP FERRAT: Hendrik Biegs